VEG&2VEG

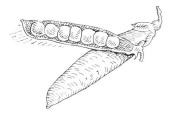

BBC BOOKS

Cecilia Norman is an established cookery writer whose best-selling book *The Good Housekeeping Step-by-Step Microwave Cookbook* sold over 100,000 copies. Over the past 18 years she has published many cookery books including some centred on health issues. Cecilia Norman is the Principal of The Recipe Agency in London, which devises recipes for food manufacturers and special-diet menus. She divides her time between London and Shropshire where she lives in historic Ironbridge on the banks of the River Severn.

Some other titles by Cecilia Norman:

Microwave Cooking
Vegetarian Microwave Cookbook
The Book of Grilling and Barbecues
Migraine Special Diet Book
The Gourmet Guide to Instant Preserving

Published by BBC Books,
a division of BBC Enterprises Limited,
Woodlands, 80 Wood Lane
London W12 0TT

First Published 1992
© Cecilia Norman 1992

ISBN 0 563 36358 4

Photographs by James Murphy
Styling by Jane McLish
Home Economist Allyson Birch
Illustrations © Peter Bailey
Set in 11/13pt Goudy Roman by Goodfellow & Egan Ltd, Cambridge
Printed and bound in Great Britain by Redwood Press Ltd, Melksham
Colour separations by Technik Ltd, Berkhamstead
Cover printed by Clays Ltd, St Ives Plc

ACKNOWLEDGEMENTS

I would like to thank
David Adlard of Adlard's Norwich for his recipe suggestions.
The Guild of Food Writers for their helpful interpretation of the COMA report.
Marlow Foods Ltd for information on Quorn.
The Fresh Fruit & Vegetable Information Bureau for their helpful regular bulletins on available fresh produce.
The Mushroom Growers Association for information and supply of British mushrooms.
Signora Evalina Sirotti of Vignola, Emilia Romana, Italy for taking me with her on a porcini gathering expedition with subsequent instruction on the art of drying and cooking porcini.
BCB Ltd on behalf of Brittany Prince Real Vegetables for the supply of artichokes, shallots and Shiitake.
Nexus PR on behalf of Porter Foods Co Ltd for providing me with information on chestnuts and chestnut purée.
Lakeland Plastics for microwave-suitable cookware.

References:
World Health Organisation (WHO) report 1991 Diet, Nutrition & the Prevention of Chronic Diseases
Committee on Medical Aspects of Food Policy (COMA) report Dietary Reference Values for food energy & nutrients of the UK 1991 published by HMSO
Federation of Bakers Medical Bulletin, Spring 1992
The Composition of Foods' 5th edition by McCance & Widdowson published by The Royal Society of Chemistry/MAFF

PREFACE

When I proposed the idea for this book it had been my intention to include lots of material for extra chapters. However, my editor, Heather Holden-Brown, highlighted the fact that what readers really needed was a straightforward veg and two veg book without any frills. A book which substitutes the meat in 'meat and two veg' with a vegetable main course and one where you wouldn't even notice that the recipes contain no meat, poultry or fish.

My first reaction to this suggestion was that it would be impossible to think up enough recipes, but the challenge became more and more exciting as I developed the recipes and new ideas were popping into my head both day and night. In the normal course of affairs I would have had the recipes tested by my home economist, but when my husband, who knows little about cooking, volunteered himself, I could hardly refuse. If *he* could follow the instructions and succeed then anyone could! I think I should point out that he is a reluctant vegetarian and his enjoyment in making and eating the dishes convinced me that you will enjoy them too, particularly because the 'two veg' recipes that accompany the main dishes are interesting dishes in their own right.

It is no good imagining that everyone follows a recipe exactly. Slight alterations and adjustments will make very little difference to the majority of recipes in this book. Using your own personal adaptations to my recipes could give you increased variety and many more tasty dishes, to add to the ones I have created.

CONTENTS

INTRODUCTION

We are much more aware today of the possibilities of creating delicious satisfying meals without using meat. And if you have a vegetarian in your family, you will also know how tricky it is to cater for everyone within one meal. In this book, I have tried to create appetising and healthy main course dishes with accompanying vegetables and salads for both everyday eating and informal entertaining. They are meals in the traditional 'meat-and-two-veg' mould but without the meat. Hopefully even the most ardent meat fan will find them hard to resist!

For easy reference, I have grouped my main course recipes together to help you build a meal around a central starting ingredient. You can choose a dish from the sections headed *Eggs and Cheese, Pastry and Batter, Pasta and Rice, Pulses and Beans, Quorn, Tofu and Nuts* or opt for one of my new dishes from the *Vegetable-based Main Course* section. You may already have a central ingredient that you want to use in a meal and by grouping the recipes I hope you will find it easier to choose the one you want. I have included old favourites like *Moussaka* using only vegetables and international dishes from Thailand, India, Mexico, Italy and China to create some unusual *Veg and 2 Veg* meals.

At the end of each recipe, I have made a few suggestions for accompanying vegetables. These are only intended to be useful guidelines but have been chosen to complement the main dishes' taste, texture and colour. The combination also offers a really balanced meal. Read through the recipe before you start so that you can prepare the companion vegetables and have everything ready for serving at once.

I hope *Veg and 2 Veg* will make cooking meals for your family and friends interesting and fun and let you discover the delights on offer from 'meatless' meals.

Notes on the recipes

To save time, many of the recipes in the book can be made in larger quantities and frozen for use later.

Microwave Guidelines

Microwave ovens are a real advantage. If you have one, many processes can be shortened by cooking part of the recipe in this type of oven. Vegetables work particularly well this way and a microwave can produce sauces with much less fuss and mess and, of course, less time. Do remember, though, that sauces should be stirred frequently.

Remember, too, that your cookware and utensils must be suitable for use in a microwave oven. Tight lids allow a build up of steam and possibly a nasty mess. Use a vented lid or partially cover the top of the bowl with cling film. Above all, always follow the manufacturer's instructions in your guide book.

Weights and Measures

Weights and measures in the recipes are given in both metric and imperial. Do not mix them in any one recipe. As a rule when metric measurements are used the finished dishes will be slightly smaller. British standard measuring spoons are recommended and all spoons are level unless otherwise stated.

Notes on the Ingredients

Butter or **margarine**   Where there is an option offered you may choose either. Where butter only is given in the ingredients list, the flavour will be less than perfect using margarine, but the dish will still be acceptable.

Canned vegetables   With the exception of baby sweet corn, most of these have a softer texture as a result of being completely cooked during the canning process. This can also cause colour change. Make sure to weigh or measure the contents after straining. I have found some staggering differences between different brands, in particular, green beans.

Cheese   Differs in fat content according to its type and, except for the soft varieties, may be manufactured using animal rennet. Popular cheeses such as Edam and Cheddar that don't contain animal rennet can be obtained fairly easily for strictly observant vegetarians.

Dried beans, peas or pulses   Where a recipe uses dried beans or peas they can be soaked and cooked at home. But why not take advantage of the excellent cans now available? These, though more expensive than dried varieties, can more than make up for the cost by the saved cost of fuel, labour, time and hassle. Other pulses such as lentils and split peas are faster to cook and often better than canned alternatives but both varieties are equally full of protein and fibre.

Flour   Plain flour can be converted to self-raising by adding baking powder, but do use the quantities advised by the manufacturers.

Frozen vegetables   Because of advances in freezing methods, these are now as nutritious as fresh vegetables. Frozen peas are now considered respectable and worth serving to even the most eminent guest, but when fresh are in season do use them as they are a real treat and taste quite different. Cook frozen vegetables without pre-thawing to sustain the texture. Some frozen vegetables such as carrots do undergo a texture change during cooking and this is perfectably acceptable in stews and casseroles. When vegetables are going to be pre-fried or sautéed it is better to use fresh ones.

Garlic   This is not to everyone's liking. In many recipes it can be reduced or omitted according to preference.

Herbs   I have no hesitation in saying that fresh herbs are far, far better than dried ones. They are certainly obtainable from most supermarkets. My second choice would be frozen herbs but if this too is out of the question, then please use only recently packed dried herbs whose colours are bright and distinct and certainly not ones that seem powdery. About one teaspoon of dried herbs equals one tablespoon of fresh or frozen, so remember to adjust quantities if you are using dried herbs. The quantities I have given are for fresh herbs unless otherwise stated.

Milk   Unless otherwise stated, milk used in the recipes is skimmed. This is so much healthier!

Nuts   These contain plenty of protein and, with the exception of coconut, polyunsaturated fat. They also contain fibre, A and B vitamins and several mineral elements including calcium and iron. Use shelled nuts soon after purchase, or store in the refrigerator or freezer to prevent them from becoming rancid. Peanuts are not nuts at all as they grow in pods under the soil rather than in shells, hence the term groundnuts.

Oils   An assortment of these have been used to produce individual flavours. Olive oil is rich in monounsaturates and sunflower oil is a polyunsaturate. Substitution will definitely affect flavours. Oil that has been used for frying becomes hydrogenated and I prefer to use a smaller amount in a smaller pan and fry a little at a time. That way there is less wastage. Drain cooked food thoroughly to remove the excess and spoon away surplus fat after frying onions before adding any remaining ingredients.

Onions   These can vary a lot in weight but as a guideline, read approximately 10 g (½ oz) for a baby onion, 25 g (1 oz) for a small one, 200 g (7 oz) for a large onion and 350 g (12 oz) for a Spanish onion.

11

Pastry   Pastry is superb when made by a light-handed cook but the attraction of the frozen packet is hard to resist. The quality is good and it can be kept in the home freezer compartment according to the storage instructions provided. Check the label to ascertain what type of fat it contains.

Reconstituted foods   Should the need arise, these can be used. Reconstituted potato in place of fresh potatoes and other convenience foods like batter mixes, pastry mixes, tomato ketchup and sauce mixes can save time, and provided you are happy with the preservatives and additives they contain, sometimes necessity dictates their usage.

Salt   A substitute can take the place of salt except in those cases where this could be harmful as it would for people with kidney problems.

Stock   Where stock is required be sure to make it from vegetables if it is to be served to vegetarians. De-fatted home-made bone stock is pleasantly glutinous and does not detract from the health aspect. Stock cubes are a helpful stand-by and these are available with both vegetable and meat content. I have not specified which to use in the list of ingredients for the recipe as the choice will lie with you, depending on who you are feeding. Some cubes are more concentrated than others and the amount of water needed will be printed on the wrapping.

Tomatoes   A medium tomato weighs approximately 75 g (3 oz), a large tomato 150 g (6 oz) not to be confused with beef tomatoes which are about 275 g (10 oz). Bear this in mind in some of the recipes.

Yogurt   This should always be natural or unflavoured. Yogurt may be made with skimmed or full cream milk, which usually comes from cows. Some yogurt is set with gelatine which is derived from the bones of animals and so is not suitable for the true vegetarian. Greek-style yogurt may be made from the milk of the ewe or buffalo and sometimes has added cream. It is imperative to read the labels. I have chosen the one that will give the best results, but if for health or ethical reasons my choice is not suitable, a substitute can be used. Home-made or commercial natural yogurt will curdle if overheated, unless it is added to a very thick sauce containing cornflour. Greek-style yogurt heats without the same problems and the texture and flavour are nearer to cream.

THE MAIN COURSE

Devising main course dishes to take the place of the 'meat' in the more traditional meal of 'meat and two veg', was quite a feat. Knowing how great an influence these will have on anyone trying vegetarian food for the first time and the importance of persuading the 'never will I eat that insipid vegetarian food again' people to change their minds, I deliberately omitted the soya bean and Textured Vegetable Protein. These are highly nutritious but for some reason they do seem to put people off. My recipes are designed to look attractive and smell and taste delicious.

The range of main course ideas is extensive, from *Tacos Mexicana* to *Savoury Roly Poly*, from *Vegetable Curry with Banana Sambal* to *French Bean, Cauliflower and Red Pepper Roulade* and from *Slatted Pasties with Leek Purée* to *Dijon Tomato Tarte*. For easy reference I have divided the recipes into groups to indicate the source ingredient and give you guidance in choosing your main courses. There is something to appeal to everyone. Some of the dishes are more elaborate and suitable for entertaining, while others are confirmed family favourites. Some are quick and easy to cook and others need more time and patience. Make your choice from these, before moving on to select the accompanying vegetables or salads.

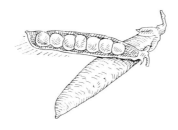

Vegetable-based Main Courses

AUTUMN COBBLER

SERVES 4–6

This is a delicious crisp cobbler-topped vegetable pie which has the added advantage of using economical ingredients.

3 medium leeks, trimmed and thickly sliced
6 shallots, peeled and halved
225 g (8 oz) parsnips, peeled and cut into chunks
175 g (6 oz) Brussels sprouts, trimmed and halved
1 stick celery, finely sliced
1 baking-size potato, peeled and cut into 8 chunks
1 small cooked beetroot, peeled and cut into small chunks
¼ stock cube, crumbled

2 tablespoons soy or bottled fruity sauce (e.g. HP or Daddies)
1 teaspoon hazelnut oil
1 tablespoon flour
freshly ground black pepper

Topping ....
175 g (6 oz) self-raising flour
½ teaspoon salt
25 g (1 oz) butter or margarine
75 g (3 oz) Cheddar cheese, grated
1 egg, beaten with 3 tablespoons milk

Pre-heat the oven to gas mark 6, 400°F (200°C).

With the exception of the beetroot, cook the vegetables in 600 ml (1 pint) boiling salted water for 10 minutes or until crisp-cooked.

Strain, reserving 150 ml (¼ pint) of the liquid. Purée with this liquid, the beetroot, the stock cube, chosen sauce, hazelnut oil and flour and pepper to taste. Pour into a large shallow oven-proof dish and spoon in the part-cooked vegetables, seasoning well.

For the topping, rub the butter or margarine into the flour and salt. Stir in most of the cheese. Add the egg and milk. Mix to a soft dough.

Roll out to 5 mm (¼ in) thickness and cut out 4 cm (1½ in) rounds. Arrange in an overlapping pattern over the vegetables, brush with water. Sprinkle with the remaining cheese and bake for 20 minutes until the topping is golden brown.

Serve with *Saffron Rice* page 126 and *Endive and Radish Salad* page 142.

BOWER ARTICHOKES

SERVES 4

Globe artichokes should be a uniform grey-green colour. If they have darkened tips and dry-looking leaves then take my advice and leave them in the shop.

4 large globe artichokes	½ small red pepper
lemon juice	salt
100 g (4 oz) bulgar (cracked wheat)	freshly ground black pepper
3 saffron strands	25 g (1 oz) butter or margarine

Wash the artichokes. Then place sideways on a chopping board and, holding the stems, firmly slice off 1 cm (½ in) from the top to remove the spikey tips. Cut off the stems. Open out slightly and wash in cold salted water.

Place in a large pan of boiling water, adding a squeeze of lemon juice. Bring to the boil, then cover and simmer for about 45 minutes. (They can be cooked in the pressure cooker for 8–10 minutes or in the microwave for 20 minutes, turning them over once during cooking.)

While the artichokes are cooking, prepare and cook the bulgar according to the directions on the packet, but add the saffron to the water. Skin, de-seed and dice the red pepper and mix into the bulgar towards the end of cooking. Season with salt and pepper and stir in the butter until melted.

When a leaf pulls away from the globe easily, it is cooked. Drain thoroughly. Allow to cool slightly, then twist out the inner core of tiny leaves and scoop out the hairy choke with a teaspoon. Remove inner leaves, scrape away the flesh and mix with the filling. Spoon the filling into the centre of the artichokes and serve hot. If necessary they can be reheated in a steamer or the microwave.

Serve with *Warm Lemon Vinaigrette* page 136 and *Garlic Sauté Mushrooms* page 113.

BRIONY PUDDING

SERVES 4

This is a light sponge pudding which should be steamed gently to maintain texture. The ingredients list looks long but all of them are simple everyday items. Although the result is much heavier, the recipe can be cooked in the microwave on medium power for about 6–10 minutes. Left-over portions reheat successfully in the microwave in seconds.

1 egg, beaten
4–5 tablespoons milk
100 g (4 oz) fine fresh white
  breadcrumbs
50 g (2 oz) plain flour
1 teaspoon baking powder
½ teaspoon salt
freshly ground black pepper
1 tablespoon grated Parmesan

1 tablespoon tomato purée
75 g (3 oz) polyunsaturated
  margarine, melted
25 g (1 oz) flaked almonds, finely
  crushed
1 small onion, very finely chopped
2 tablespoons cooked diced carrot
2 tablespoons finely sliced celery
8 tablespoons frozen peas

Prepare a steamer (or large saucepan fitted with a rack and containing 2.5 cm (1 in) simmering water), a square of greaseproof paper and some foil. Butter a 900 ml (1½ pint) pudding basin.

Beat the egg with 4 tablespoons of the milk. Put the crumbs in a mixing bowl and sift in the flour, baking powder, salt and pepper.

Stir in the Parmesan, tomato purée, margarine and egg mixture. Fold in the nuts and vegetables. If necessary, add the remaining tablespoon of milk to form a soft dropping consistency.

Turn the mixture into the basin, cover with the greaseproof paper and a large piece of foil and seal with string. Steam the pudding in the lidded pan for 2 hours, topping up with boiling water as needed.

Turn the pudding out on to a heated serving dish and serve at once with *Creamed Spinach* page 109 and roast parsnips, and a sauce such as *Espagnole sauce* page 131, or a cheese sauce or tomato sauce.

BRITTANY ARTICHOKE MIETTES

SERVES 4

When large Brittany artichokes are in season, there are none better. If you can't find fresh artichokes you can use canned artichoke bottoms. A 400 g (14 oz) can usually contains eight.

16 cooked or canned artichoke
  bottoms

Filling ....
40 g (1½ oz) butter or margarine
1 medium onion, chopped
1 leek, white part only, chopped
grated rind and juice of ½ lemon
½ teaspoon Worcestershire sauce or
  vegetarian equivalent
50 g (2 oz) fresh brown breadcrumbs
50 g (2 oz) fine oatmeal

1 tablespoon freshly chopped parsley
1 egg
salt
freshly ground black pepper

Coating ....
2 eggs beaten
8–10 tablespoons brown breadcrumbs
flour blended with cold water to a
  coating consistency
oil for deep frying

If using fresh artichokes, break off the stems, remove and set aside the outer layers of leaves. Twist off the inner leaves and cut away the hairy choke. Trim the tough core from the underside.

Melt the butter or margarine in a saucepan and fry the onion and leek until soft. Remove from the heat, then stir in lemon, Worcestershire sauce, brown breadcrumbs, oatmeal, parsley and egg. Season well. The mixture should be soft, but hold its shape so that the filling does not ooze out of the artichoke when filled.

Sandwich pairs of hollowed artichoke bottoms together with the filling and shape removing any excess filling so that the sides are smooth. Leave until cold.

Dip the artichoke sandwiches into the beaten egg, coat with the breadcrumbs, then dip in the flour paste. Deep fry until golden brown and then drain on kitchen paper.

If using fresh artichokes arrange the reserved leaves in a circle around hot dinner plates, placing the fried *Miettes* in the centre. Serve with *Creamy Hollandaise Sauce* page 130 and creamed potatoes.

CAULIFLOWER AND POTATO BHAJI

SERVES 4

This is a hot curry but it can be calmed by substituting a mild curry paste and is a drier curry with less gravy than a conventional curry – delicious! The cardamom husks are not edible, but are cooked to give flavour and can easily be pushed to the side of the plate when eating.

2 tablespoons sunflower oil
1 teaspoon hazelnut oil
1 large onion, very finely chopped
1 clove garlic, crushed lightly
12 green peppercorns
12 cardamom pods, crushed
2 tablespoons bottled hot curry paste
1 small cauliflower, divided into florets
450 g (1 lb) potatoes, peeled and cut
  into small chunks

2 tablespoons tomato purée
450 ml (¾ pint) stock
8 okra, trimmed and halved
½ teaspoon salt
half a cinnamon stick
2 tablespoons Greek-style yogurt
1 tablespoon chopped fresh coriander
  leaves.

Heat the oils in a large saucepan and fry the onion and garlic until soft.

Add the peppercorns and cardamom pods and fry, stirring for 30 seconds. Stir in the curry paste. Add the cauliflower florets and the potato a few pieces at a time and cook gently for 3–4 minutes, turning and stirring to coat them in the curry paste.

Mix in the tomato purée, stock, okra, salt and cinnamon stick. Bring to the boil, then cook over moderate heat for 20 minutes or until the cauliflower and potato are tender and the liquid is reduced to about 150 ml (¼ pint). Check that the liquid level is maintained.

Remove the cinnamon stick and stir in the yogurt just before serving. Garnish with the coriander.

Serve with *Cucumber Raita* page 140 and *Saffron Rice* page 126, or as part of a 'Curry Dinner' with *Samosas* page 70 and *Dhal* page 88.

CHARLOTTE PROVENÇALE

SERVES 4

Cook this in one large or several small shallow ovenproof dishes. This dish freezes well so you may like to put it in foil dishes which can be popped into a hot oven for 15 minutes to warm through and brown.

2 tablespoons olive oil
1 tablespoon sunflower oil
3 Spanish onions, finely sliced
450 g (1 lb) tomatoes,
  preferably skinned
12 black olives, stoned and sliced
salt
freshly ground black pepper

2 teaspoons finely scissored fresh
  thyme leaves
2 teaspoons finely scissored fresh
  tarragon leaves
75 g (3 oz) Cheddar cheese, grated
75 g–100 g (3 oz–4 oz) fresh
  wholemeal breadcrumbs

Pre-heat the oven to gas mark 5, 375°F (190°C).

Heat the oils in a large frying-pan and sauté the onions until just turning brown at the edges.

Transfer half of the onions, using a slotted spoon so you can drain off the oil, to a large shallow ovenproof dish. Cover with a layer of tomatoes and all the olives. Season with salt and pepper, add a sprinkling of the herbs and some of the cheese. Arrange the remaining onions over the top and then layer the rest of the tomatoes, cheese and herbs. Season again.

Spoon the breadcrumbs evenly over the surface and drizzle with the left over oil from the frying-pan. Place the dish in the centre of the oven and cook for 25–30 minutes until the vegetables are soft and the topping is crisp and golden brown.

Serve with *Roast Pumpkin* page 125 and Brussels sprouts.

COUSCOUS ALGÉRIEN

SERVES 4

Couscous is made from fine semolina. The tiny particles are coated with flour to produce larger grains. Pre-cooked couscous is available (in the same way as rice is obtainable pre-fluffed and lasagne pre-cooked) and this greatly speeds the cooking time but the preparation instructions on the packet should be followed. When using in place of the untreated couscous detailed in this recipe, ignore the initial 30 minutes cooking time.

450 g (1 lb) couscous
100 g (4 oz) runner beans, trimmed and sliced
100 g (4 oz) cabbage, coarsely chopped
1 red pepper, de-seeded and diced
1 large potato, cut into small chunks
1 onion, grated
1 small courgette, topped, tailed and thickly sliced

½ teaspoon ground cumin
1 green chilli, de-seeded and chopped (optional)
227 g (8 oz) can chopped tomatoes
1 tablespoon chopped pine kernels
1 tablespoon raisins
salt
freshly ground pepper
1 tablespoon olive oil

Have ready a stainless steel colander and a large saucepan on to which this will sit snugly.

Put the couscous in a bowl and add 4 tablespoons cold water, one at a time, working each in with the fingertips.

Put about 2.5 cm (1 in) water in a large saucepan and bring to the boil. Reduce the heat to simmering. Tip the couscous into the colander and place it on the saucepan, checking that the bottom of the colander does not touch the water. Steam uncovered for 30 minutes, topping up the water with more boiling water when necessary.

Remove the colander from the pan, turn the couscous into a bowl and add 4 tablespoons cold water, mixing in a little at a time with a metal spoon. Replace in the colander and steam for 30 minutes as before.

Meanwhile put all the remaining ingredients in a large saucepan, cover tightly with a lid and cook, without adding water, over moderate heat until the vegetables are tender, shaking the pan occasionally.

Stir the oil into the couscous and season with salt to taste. Turn on to a heated serving dish, top with the vegetable mixture and serve with *Egg and Cucumber Salad* page 141 and a green salad.

21

CROWN OF VEGETABLES WITH
MUSHROOM FILLING

SERVES 4

An attractive ring of mixed vegetables served hot with a filling of creamed mushrooms. This can be prepared and assembled in advance to be baked when required but if starting from cold a little extra baking time will be needed.

225 g (8 oz) broccoli florets
175 g (6 oz) cauliflower florets
salt
1 large carrot, sliced
1 red pepper, de-seeded and diced
12 fresh chives, finely scissored
freshly ground black pepper
8 tablespoons mayonnaise

Mushroom Filling ....
25 g (1 oz) butter or margarine
350 g (12 oz) mushrooms, very finely
   sliced
25 g (1 oz) fresh granary breadcrumbs
250 ml (8 fl oz) Greek-style yogurt
2 teaspoons fresh lemon juice
15 g (½ oz) ground almonds
150 ml (¼ pint) milk

Pre-heat the oven to gas mark 5, 375°F (190°C).

Cook the broccoli and cauliflower in a minimum of boiling salted water in a tightly lidded pan for about 3 minutes, until crisp-cooked. Remove the vegetables with a slotted spoon, place in a colander and cool under cold running water to prevent further softening. Drain thoroughly.

Add the carrot and pepper to the pan with extra boiling water if necessary and cook and drain in the same way.

Spread the chives in the base of a buttered 1 litre (1¾ pint) ring mould and pack the cooked vegetables in very tightly, arranging them in an attractive design around the base and sides, alternating the colours and season to taste as you do so.

Spoon the mayonnaise over the surface. Cover with foil and place on a baking tray and bake for 15–20 minutes until thoroughly heated.

Melt the butter or margarine in a pan and sauté the mushrooms for 5 minutes, seasoning well. Stir in the breadcrumbs and cook for 1–2 minutes. Mix in the yogurt, lemon juice, ground almonds and milk. Reduce the heat and stir for about 1 minute to heat but not cook.

Remove the foil from the vegetable ring and carefully invert on to a heated platter. Fill the centre with the mushroom mixture and serve hot with *Tabbouleh* page 149 and a tomato salad.

FENNEL TOSCANA

SERVES 4

Fennel has a pungent aniseed flavour which abates when it is cooked. It is said to be very good for the digestion and once having acquired a taste for it, this vegetable becomes a must. I have named the recipe Toscana because of my wonderful memories of a Christmas spent in Pietrasanta in Tuscany, where I first tasted it.

2 medium-size fennel bulbs	225 g (8 oz) ricotta cheese
salt	freshly ground black pepper
2 Italian plum tomatoes	¼ teaspoon ground allspice

Wash the fennel and remove the tips of the stalks and coarse outer leaves. Halve lengthwise and cook in boiling salted water for 25 minutes or until tender. Remove with a slotted spoon.

Immerse the tomatoes in the pan of boiling water for one minute, then skin and chop.

Pour away most of the water from the pan, leaving about 2.5 cm (1 in) and reheat until boiling, then remove the pan from the heat.

Put the ricotta into a small bowl, mash and stand in the pan of hot water. Stir gently until soft. Season with salt and pepper and mix in the allspice.

Pile the ricotta on to the flat surface of the fennel and place a line of chopped tomato down each centre. Arrange in a single layer on the grill rack and lightly brown under moderate heat.

Serve as a main dish with *Pommes Amandine* page 121 and *Garlic Sauté Mushrooms* page 113.

FRENCH BEAN, CAULIFLOWER AND RED PEPPER ROULADE

SERVES 4

There's no denying that the thought of making a roulade is daunting but it becomes easy once you get the hang of it. Make the filling ahead of time if it is more convenient or do it in the microwave using a 2 litre (3½ pint) bowl and save your energy for the souffléed part.

Filling ....
40 g (1½ oz) butter or margarine
2 spring onions, trimmed and
  finely sliced
225 g (8 oz) French beans, trimmed
  and finely sliced
1 small red pepper, de-seeded and
  finely chopped
40 g (1½ oz) plain flour
300 ml (½ pint) milk
salt
freshly ground black pepper
175 g (6 oz) cauliflower florets,
  chopped

50 g (2 oz) Lancashire cheese,
  crumbled

Base ....
5 large eggs, separated
150 ml (¼ pint) Greek-style yogurt
½ teaspoon paprika
50 g (2 oz) fresh breadcrumbs
100 g (4 oz) grated Gruyère cheese
freshly ground black pepper
¼ teaspoon salt
....
25 g (1 oz) ground almonds

To make the filling, melt the butter or margarine in a large saucepan, add the spring onions, French beans and red pepper and cook over moderate heat, stirring continuously until soft.

Mix in the flour, then gradually stir in the milk and continue cooking until the vegetables are in a thick sauce. Season with salt and pepper.

Add the cauliflower and cheese, cover with a lid and cook over a low heat for 5 minutes, stirring from time to time. Cover and set aside.

To prepare the roulade line a 23 cm × 33 cm (9 in × 13 in) Swiss roll tin with non-stick parchment large enough to protrude above the rim (a smear of butter or margarine will help secure it in position).

Pre-heat the oven to gas mark 6, 400°F (200°C).

In a large bowl beat the egg yolks, yogurt and paprika with a fork, then mix in the breadcrumbs, Gruyère and a generous shake of black pepper.

Put the egg whites and salt in a clean bowl and beat with a whisk until stiff but not dry. Stir a quarter of this into the yogurt mixture to loosen it a little, then fold in the remainder with a large metal spoon.

Pour but do not spoon the mixture into the prepared tin and tip the tin to encourage the mixture to reach the corners. Smooth the top gently with a palette knife.

Bake in the centre of the oven for 15 minutes until just set and the surface is a pale golden brown.

Meanwhile reheat the filling, adding a little milk to the mixture to keep the consistency spreadable.

Cut a sheet of non-stick parchment a little larger than the tin lining and spread with the ground almonds.

Remove the tin from the oven when the base is ready. Courageously grasp one long edge of the lining around the roulade base and flip the roulade over on to the ground almonds.

Remove the lining parchment from the roulade, spread the filling over the roulade while hot, to within 2.5 cm (1 in) of the long edges. With the aid of the parchment you have turned the roulade on to, roll up from the lower edge. Squeeze gently to shape nicely, then take away the parchment.

Serve at once with sauté potatoes and a green salad.

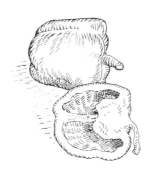

GRUYÈRE AND CORN RELISH CROQUETTES

SERVES 4

The secret of success in this recipe is in the chilling, which firms up the mixture and so prevents the breaking up of the croquettes during cooking. I used the corn chutney from my Gourmet Guide to Instant Preserves but any variety containing whole corn kernels will suffice.

500 g (1 lb) floury potatoes, boiled
25 g (1 oz) butter or margarine
2 egg yolks
salt
freshly ground black pepper
100 g (4 oz) Gruyère cheese,
  finely grated

flour
4 tablespoons corn chutney
beaten egg
8–12 tablespoons fresh finely grated
  breadcrumbs
oil for frying

Mash the warm potatoes with the butter and work in the egg yolks, salt and pepper to taste. Mix in the cheese, then refrigerate until cold.

Divide the mixture into eight portions and shape into 9 cm × 5 cm (3½ in × 2 in) rectangles on a floured surface. Place a little of the chutney along the centre, lift the longer edges up and press together to seal, then press in the sides to completely enclose the filling and shape into croquettes.

Dip the croquettes in the beaten egg and coat with the breadcrumbs and deep fry for about 1–2 minutes, making sure that the croquettes are fully immersed. Remove with a slotted spoon, drain quickly on kitchen paper.

Serve at once with *Ratatouille* page 122 and *Spicy Spinach* page 127.

KILLARNEY PIE

SERVES 4–6

Many interesting and economical recipes originate from Ireland and there are a lot of variations. I have adapted this from a recipe given to me by an Irish friend, to improve its nutritional value.

1 kg (2 lb) large floury potatoes
  e.g. King Edward or Maris Piper
3 large carrots
1 small swede
2 large parsnips
1–2 tablespoons milk
50 g (2 oz) butter or margarine

salt
freshly ground black pepper
200 g (7 oz) cooked or canned borlotti
  beans, drained and rinsed
3 tablespoons creamed horseradish
3 tablespoons mayonnaise
3–4 tablespoons fresh breadcrumbs

Pre-heat the oven to gas mark 6, 400°F (200°C).

Prepare the vegetables, cutting the potatoes into chunks and dicing the carrots, swede and parsnips.

Boil the potatoes in salted water until tender but do not overcook them. Drain, then mash with the milk, half the butter or margarine and season to taste with salt and pepper.

Cook the other vegetables together in boiling salted water until just tender. Drain and reserve the liquid. Add the beans, then fold in the horseradish sauce, mayonnaise and 8 tablespoons of the reserved liquid. Season to taste with salt and pepper.

Spoon the mixed vegetables into a baking dish and spread the mashed potato on top. Sprinkle with the breadcrumbs and dot with the remaining butter.

Bake for 45–50 minutes until crisp and brown on top.

Serve with *Quick Tomato Sauce* page 133 or *Espagnole Sauce* page 131, freshly steamed Brussels sprouts and *Crispy Onion Rings* page 110.

LINCOLNSHIRE CRUMBLE

SERVES 4

Choosing potatoes is like wandering through a veritable maze, there are so many kinds available from the home-grown to the imported. In most supermarkets they are labelled. For this recipe I would recommend maincrop King Edwards which are less likely to discolour and have a lovely floury texture.

175 g (6 oz) wholemeal flour
75 g (3 oz) butter or hard margarine,
  diced
50 g (2 oz) grated Parmesan cheese
salt
freshly ground black pepper
2 large baking potatoes,
  peeled and sliced

1 egg, beaten
3–4 tablespoons olive oil
2 medium red onions, sliced
1 small aubergine, peeled and sliced
4 medium tomatoes, sliced
225 g (½ lb) vegetable marrow,
  peeled, de-seeded and sliced

Pre-heat the oven to gas mark 5, 375°F (190°C).

Put the flour into a mixing bowl, add the butter and rub in until the mixture resembles fine crumbs. Stir in 25 g (1 oz) of the Parmesan and season with salt and pepper.

Partially cook the potatoes in boiling salted water for about 5 minutes. Drain thoroughly, leave to cool, then dip in the egg and coat thoroughly with the crumbs. Spread out on a tray and refrigerate until required.

Heat 2 tablespoons of the oil in a large frying-pan and fry the onion until soft. Add the aubergine and continue frying until only just brown, adding more oil as necessary.

Remove the vegetables from the pan and layer with the tomato and marrow in a buttered baking dish, seasoning each layer lightly with salt and pepper and scatter with the remaining Parmesan. Moisten with a few tablespoons of water.

Top with overlapping slices of the crumbed potato and bake for 25–30 minutes until the potatoes are crunchy.

Serve with *Hot Beetroot Salad* page 144 and green peas.

MIXED GRILL

SERVES 4

This recipe is fairly quick and easy to prepare. It helps to choose larger vegetables, and place the pan well below the element to get the best results.

8 slices French bread, 3 cm (1¼ in) thick
6–7 tablespoons olive oil
salt
freshly ground pepper
4 tablespoons minced onion
½ tablespoon fresh lemon juice
1 teaspoon French mustard
4 artichoke bottoms, cooked or canned
2 large tomatoes, halved
4 large flat mushrooms

Arrange the bread in a single layer in a foil-lined grill pan. Spoon 2 teaspoons of oil over each slice, allow to soak in, then season with salt and pepper.

Top with the onion and press hard with a fork to impregnate, so preventing the onion from toppling off when turned over.

Mix the lemon juice, mustard and 1 tablespoon of the oil, season well and brush over both sides of the artichoke bottoms. Place in the grill pan next to the bread slices.

Add to the grill pan the tomatoes and the mushrooms flat side up. Season sparingly and sprinkle with oil.

Grill under moderate heat, turning the bread to toast on both sides. Transfer to heated plates as the various items are ready.

Serve with oven chips or steamed new potatoes, *Medley of Green Beans* page 117 and fried eggs if desired.

MOUSSAKA

SERVES 4

Moussaka or moussakas as it is usually described in its homeland, has always been a mainstay of the Greek and Cypriot diet. Originally consisting of layers of sliced vegetables and spicy minced meat topped with a souffléed white sauce, this dish has become universally popular and subject to endless adaptations. My vegetable version is as tasty as the original and so much less greasy than many meat-based ones.

1 medium aubergine, topped,
  tailed and thinly sliced
2 medium courgettes, thinly sliced
salt
450 g (1 lb) large potatoes, peeled
  and thinly sliced
freshly ground black pepper
2 tablespoons chopped fresh
  oregano leaves
2–3 tablespoons olive oil

Lentil and tomato sauce ....
400 g (14 oz) can chopped tomatoes
1 tablespoon tomato purée
1 medium onion, finely chopped

2 stock cubes
100 g (4 oz) red split lentils,
  well rinsed
5 tablespoons dry white wine

White sauce ....
600 ml (1 pint) milk
3 tablespoons sunflower oil
4 tablespoons plain flour
75 g (3 oz) grated Parmesan cheese
pinch nutmeg
2 large eggs, beaten
salt
white pepper

Sprinkle the aubergine and courgettes with salt and leave for 30 minutes. Rinse, drain and pat dry with a clean tea cloth.

Pre-heat the oven to gas mark 6, 400°F (200°C).

Layer the potatoes, courgettes and aubergines in a large baking dish, seasoning each layer with salt and pepper and sprinkling with oregano and olive oil.

Cover tightly with buttered foil and bake for 25–35 minutes until the vegetables are soft.

Meanwhile prepare the sauces. Mix the lentil and tomato sauce ingredients in one large saucepan. Add 900 ml (1½ pints) boiling water, bring to the boil, then reduce the heat and simmer uncovered for 20 minutes or until the mixture is reduced to a thick sauce.

In another pan blend the milk, sunflower oil and flour together and cook over moderate heat, stirring continuously until thickened to the consistency of pouring cream. Remove from the heat, leave for a few minutes, then beat in the Parmesan and nutmeg followed by the eggs. Season with salt and pepper.

Spoon the lentil mixture over the vegetables in the baking dish and cover with the white sauce. Return to the oven and bake for 25 minutes or until the top is brown. Alternatively you could heat and brown this dish under a moderate grill.

Serve with *Feta and Black Olive Salad* page 142 and a mixed salad.

MUSHY PEA AND PARSLEY ROULADE

SERVES 4

A simpler version of the roulade. The creamy mushy pea filling is wonderful as it is, but can be dressed up by adding chopped pistachios and pine nuts and a touch of chopped rosemary. Dare I admit that my family like it mixed with chopped baked oven chips?

75 g (3 oz) soft margarine
65 g (2½ oz) plain flour
600 ml (1 pint) milk
salt
freshly ground black pepper

6 eggs, separated
2 tablespoons freshly chopped parsley
400 g (14 oz) can mushy peas, drained
6–8 tablespoons fine breadcrumbs,
  toasted

Generously butter a 30 cm × 18 cm (12 in × 7 in) baking tin and line the base with non-stick parchment.

Pre-heat the oven to gas mark 7, 425°F (220°C).

Put the margarine, flour and milk in a saucepan. Whisk continuously over a moderate heat until sauce thickens. Season with salt and pepper and continue cooking over low heat for 3–4 minutes.

Pour two-thirds of the sauce into a large bowl and whisk in the egg yolks and parsley. Stir the mushy peas into the sauce remaining in the pan and warm over low heat.

Using clean beaters whisk the egg whites to soft peaks. Stir 2 tablespoons of the whites into the yolk mixture, then fold in the remainder with a large metal spoon. Turn into the prepared tin, and without using undue pressure smooth the surface with a palette knife.

Bake for 10–15 minutes until risen and springy on top.

Meanwhile cut a large sheet of non-stick paper, slightly larger than the baking tray, and sprinkle with most of the breadcrumbs. Turn the roulade base on to the crumbs and strip away the lining paper.

Trim away any crispy edges, spread the mushy pea filling over the surface leaving a 5 cm (2 in) border at one short side. Roll up from the other short side, using the parchment to help as a guide and prevent the delicate roulade from sticking to the fingers. Squeeze the roll gently into shape and scatter with the rest of the breadcrumbs.

Serve the roulade with *Peanut and Gem Lettuce Salad* page 147 and *Fantailed Potatoes* page 111 (which will not suffer if the oven temperature is raised during the last 15 minutes to accommodate the roulade).

ORANGE FLAVOURED STUFFED MARROW

SERVES 4

Marrows can be straight, curvy, uneven and of different diameters and up to about 27 kg (60 lb) in weight! For this recipe select a medium-size straight marrow about 10 cm (4 in) diameter.

1 medium marrow
grated zest and juice of 2 large oranges
salt
freshly ground black pepper
generous pinch ground ginger
1 medium carrot, sliced
1 small onion, very finely chopped

2 tablespoons tomato purée
dash of Tabasco
4 tablespoons fresh brown
  breadcrumbs
350 g (12 oz) cooked or canned butter
  beans, mashed
butter or margarine

Pre-heat the oven to gas mark 5, 375°F (190°C).

Top, tail and peel the marrow. Cut crosswise into four cylinders of equal length.

Put marrow into a large saucepan with the orange juice and season with salt and pepper. Cover tightly with the lid and cook over gentle heat for 10–15 minutes until just tender.

Remove the marrow with a slotted spoon and put the ginger, carrot and onion in the pan. Cover with the lid and simmer for 5 minutes.

Mix in the orange zest, tomato purée, Tabasco, breadcrumbs and butter beans. Crush with a potato masher, adjust the seasoning and add 1–2 tablespoons water if needed. The mixture should be firm but not hard.

Scoop out the seeds from the marrow and stuff the hollows with the orange mixture. Stand them in a buttered baking tin. Dot with butter or margarine and bake for 25–35 minutes.

Serve with *Quick Tomato Sauce* page 133, *Paprika Potatoes* page 118 and *Toujours Cauliflower* page 129.

33

POTATO GNOCCHI

SERVES 4–6

Gnocchi is Italian for small tubular shaped dumplings. They may be made from potato, flour or semolina, and Parmesan features in most recipes. This is a basic recipe which I make when short of time.

1 kg (2 lb) maincrop potatoes, peeled and cut into chunks
salt
freshly ground black pepper
40 g (1½ oz) butter or margarine
2 eggs, beaten

2 tablespoons grated Parmesan cheese
225–275 g (8–10 oz) plain flour
6–8 tablespoons *Pesto*, bottled or home-made page 132
extra Parmesan

Cook the potatoes in boiling salted water until tender. Drain thoroughly and mash, making sure no lumps are left. Season with salt and pepper. While still hot mix in the butter or margarine until melted, add the eggs, Parmesan and as much flour as is needed to hold the mixture together.

With floured hands shape spoonsful of the mixture into barrels to approximately 2.5 cm (1 in) long and 1 cm (½ in) thick.

Heat a pan of lightly salted boiling water. Using a slotted spoon add the gnocchi a few at a time, transferring them to a buttered casserole dish as soon as they rise to the surface. Cover and keep warm.

Warm the Pesto. Spoon over the gnocchi and sprinkle with extra Parmesan cheese. Allow 12–15 gnocchi per portion.

Serve with *Medley of Green Beans* page 117 and *Red Pepper Compôte* page 123.

RICH BROWN CASSEROLE

◆

SERVES 4

Slow cooking is the reason for the success of this recipe. It is also a recipe that can be adapted but you must keep watch on the liquid level, adding more stock when needed.

50 g (2 oz) butter or margarine
45 g (1¾ oz) plain flour
450 ml (¾ pint) well-flavoured stock
250 ml (8 fl oz) medium red wine
salt
freshly ground pepper
400 g (14 oz) can baked beans in
   tomato sauce
1 teaspoon fresh lemon juice
½ teaspoon fennel seeds

3 bay leaves
450 g (1 lb) floury potatoes, e.g. King
   Edward or Maris Piper, peeled and
   cut into chunks
1 large carrot, sliced
2 medium onions, finely sliced
2 sticks celery, sliced
3 open mushrooms, chopped
4–6 baby sweet corn

Melt the butter in a frying pan or large flameproof casserole dish, stir in the flour and, stirring continuously, cook over low heat for 5 minutes until beige.

Gradually stir in the stock and wine and cook over moderate heat, still stirring, until the sauce is thick enough to coat the back of a wooden spoon. Season with salt and pepper.

If using a frying-pan transfer the sauce to a casserole, otherwise complete the dish in the same casserole. Stir in the baked beans, their sauce and the remaining ingredients.

Cover the dish with buttered foil before putting on the lid and bake at gas mark 3, 325°F (160°C) for 2 hours, stirring occasionally to mix in any thickened sauce around the sides. Reduce the temperature to gas mark 2, 300°F (150°C) and cook for a further hour. Remove the bay leaves.

Serve with plain cooked shredded cabbage and warmed *Tricorn Puffs* page 156.

ROAST AUBERGINE PROVENÇALE

SERVES 4–6

Over-large aubergines tend to have tougher skins than the smaller ones and these skins may not be edible. Choose the firm shiny unwrinkled kind.

4 medium aubergines
salt
2–3 tablespoons vegetable oil
1 medium onion, chopped
1 clove garlic, crushed
2 heaped tablespoons fresh wholemeal breadcrumbs
1 teaspoon chopped fresh basil leaves
1 tablespoon tomato purée

freshly ground black pepper
4 tomatoes, sliced
1 heaped tablespoon grated mature Cheddar cheese
1 level tablespoon grated Parmesan cheese
1 level tablespoon freshly chopped parsley

Pre-heat the oven to gas mark 4, 350°F (180°C).

Halve the aubergines lengthways, score the flesh with a sharp knife, criss-cross fashion, and sprinkle generously with salt. Place cut side down on a baking tray and leave for at least 30 minutes to remove the bitter juices which the salt will draw out.

Rinse thoroughly under cold running water. Pat dry with kitchen paper. Scoop out the flesh leaving a 5 mm (¼ in) wall. Dice the flesh and cook gently in the oil until tender. Add the onion and garlic to the pan and continue cooking until the onion softens. Remove the pan from the heat and mix in the breadcrumbs, basil, tomato purée and a generous shake of pepper.

Pile the mixture into the aubergine shells, cover with the tomato slices and top with the mixed cheeses. Place in a single layer in a roasting dish and bake for 25–30 minutes until beginning to brown on top.

Garnish with the parsley. Serve with *Pommes Amandine* page 121 and plain cooked green beans.

SALADE TOUT PRÊT

SERVES 4

This is almost a store-cupboard recipe as you may well have most of the ingredients to hand already. Radicchio has a texture which is more like cabbage than lettuce and as a result wilts less quickly, and can be kept much longer.

100 g (4 oz) cooked or canned
 broad beans
100 g (4 oz) cooked or canned
 chick peas
25 g (1 oz) salted peanuts
1 tablespoon capers, chopped
4 hard-boiled eggs, chopped

1 small Radicchio, shredded
3 tablespoons olive oil
2 tablespoons red wine vinegar
salt
freshly ground black pepper
3 tablespoons chopped fresh parsley

Put the beans, chick peas, peanuts, capers, eggs and Radicchio together in a salad bowl.

Blend the oil and vinegar and season sparingly with salt and pepper. Pour over the salad ingredients and toss to coat evenly. Sprinkle with the parsley just before serving.

Serve with *Hot Cheese Waffles* page 154, potato salad and cold *Rice Pimiento Castles* page 124.

SOUTH AFRICAN POTJIE

SERVES 6–8

In South Africa the concept of cooking outside is popular and, although the braai or barbecue is much quicker, there is something appealing in sitting around waiting for the pot to cook. A potjie is a cast iron cooking pot on three legs. The pot is filled with casserole ingredients, the lid fitted tightly and set over a small fire. This slow cooking brings out the flavours which mingle and cook in a minimum of liquid, thus producing a rich flavoursome sauce. Here in the UK the recipe can be cooked in a low oven or slow cooker. It can be frozen and reheated if wished.

1 small celeriac
generous squeeze fresh lemon juice
1 small aubergine
salt
4 large onions, sliced
2 pickled walnuts, chopped
175 g (6 oz) long grain rice
1 medium swede, peeled and cubed
1 green pepper, de-seeded and cut
 into rings

450 g (1 lb) ripe tomatoes, thickly
 sliced
freshly ground black pepper
1 tablespoon chopped fresh marjoram
3 baking size potatoes, peeled and cut
 into 2 cm (1 in) thick slices
450 ml (¾ pint) medium white wine
2 teaspoons Marmite or similar yeast
 extract
½ stock cube
flour for paste

Peel and cube the celeriac and immerse in water with the lemon juice to prevent discoloration.

Slice the aubergine, spread out on a deep plate and sprinkle liberally with salt. Leave for 20 minutes.

Drain the celeriac, rinse and drain the aubergine.

Arrange the onions in the base of a large casserole and cover with the pickled walnuts and rice.

Layer all the remaining vegetables except the potatoes in the dish, seasoning well with salt and pepper and a sprinkling of marjoram. Top with the potatoes, then pour over the wine.

Dissolve the Marmite and stock cube in 300 ml (10 fl oz) hot water, add to the dish and cover with the lid.

Make a thick paste with flour and water and brush round the joins of the lid and base of the dish to make sure of a perfect seal. Do not forget to seal the hole in the lid if there is one. Place the casserole in the lower part of the oven.

Bake at gas mark 3, 325°F (160°C) for 2 hours.

Remove the lid, chipping away the paste seal and check that both the rice and vegetables are cooked and most of the liquid has been absorbed. If needed add more water or wine. Adjust the seasoning, replace the lid and continue cooking if necessary.

Serve with canned baked beans and cabbage or spring greens.

STUFFED FIELD MUSHROOMS

SERVES 4

Field mushrooms (Agaricus campestris) can vary between 3–10 cm (1¼–4 in) across and it is the largest of these that are most suited to this recipe. The open cap mushrooms haven't the meaty nature or the domed feature of a field mushroom. If you cannot obtain this variety use the large flat kind.

4 large field mushrooms
1 tablespoon olive oil
freshly ground black pepper
225 g (8 oz) mashed potato

3 tablespoons fromage frais
2 tablespoons chopped fresh parsley
4 tablespoons grated Cheddar cheese

Pre-heat the oven to gas mark 5, 375°F (190°C).

Cut off the mushroom stalks close to the gills and chop them finely. Wipe the mushroom caps and peel only if needed. Arrange gill side up in a single layer in a buttered baking dish. Sprinkle with the oil and season well with pepper.

Bake for 15 minutes until still firm yet only partly cooked.

Meanwhile thoroughly mix the reserved stalks, potato, fromage frais and parsley together with a fork (not the food processor). Pile on to the mushroom caps, smooth with a table knife, then ridge with a fork. Sprinkle with the Cheddar cheese.

Return the stuffed mushrooms to the oven and bake for 20–25 minutes until the potato stuffing is thoroughly hot and brown on top.

Serve with *Soured Cream Gravy* page 134, *Roast Pumpkin* page 125 and *Savoy Cabbage and Tomato Fricassée* page 126.

SPRING GREEN DOLMADES – GEMMA'S CHOICE

SERVES 4

Large leaves of spring greens, blanched and stuffed with mashed potato, shallots, celeriac and salted peanuts, scattered with cheese and baked in a hot oven and made even more exciting when served with Mustard Sauce page 132. To save time instant potato could be used.

1 bunch of spring greens	½ teaspoon paprika
2 shallots, very finely chopped or grated	1 teaspoon polyunsaturated margarine
50 g (2 oz) salted peanuts, finely chopped	salt
100 g (4 oz) piece of peeled celeriac	freshly ground black pepper
225 g (8 oz) mashed potato	175 ml (6 fl oz) stock
	40 g (1½ oz) grated Cheddar cheese

Pre-heat the oven to gas mark 4, 350°F (180°C).

Separate the outer darker leaves of the greens and discard any that are badly blemished. Plunge into a saucepan of boiling water and cook for no longer than 2 minutes. Place in a colander under cold running water until all the leaves are cool. Drain thoroughly.

Shred the inner leaves finely and put in a bowl with the shallots and peanuts. Coarsely grate, then add the celeriac. Mix well.

Thoroughly mix the potato, paprika and margarine evenly. Add seasoning to taste.

Lay the cooked dark leaves individually on a chopping board and cut out the thick stems. Cross the open ends of the leaves over one another. Spread the potato in the centre of each leaf and cover with the shredded vegetables and nuts.

Roll up the leaves, folding in the sides to enclose the filling and arrange in a single layer in a well buttered shallow casserole dish. Pour over the stock. Cover and bake for 20–30 minutes.

Sprinkle the cheese over the rolls and raise the oven temperature to gas mark 6, 400°F (200°C) for a further 15 minutes uncovered.

Serve hot with a spoon of *Mustard Sauce* page 132 on the side of the plates with freshly cooked vermicelli and *Baked Tomatoes* page 106.

SUNSHINE CAULIFLOWER

SERVES 4

Cauliflower is obtainable all year round although prices can fluctuate alarmingly. This vegetable does not withstand overcooking. Never leave cauliflower in a covered pan after it is cooked, as carry-over cooking continues in the trapped heat.

1 medium cauliflower	freshly ground black pepper
50 g (2 oz) butter or margarine	150 g (5 oz) frozen peas
50 g (2 oz) plain flour	75 g (3 oz) cooked or canned
600 ml (1 pint) milk	chick peas
75 g (3 oz) grated mature	75 g (3 oz) cornflakes,
Cheddar cheese	coarsely crushed

Pre-heat the oven to gas mark 7, 425°F (220°C).

Remove the outer leaves and tough core from the base of the cauliflower. Carefully cut out the florets and cook in boiling salted water until crisp-cooked. Drain through a colander and refresh under cold running water.

To make the sauce, melt the butter in a saucepan, stir in the flour and cook over moderate heat stirring continuously for 1 minute. Add the milk and beat continuously until smooth. Mix in the cheese and black pepper and remove the pan from the heat.

Dip the florets in the sauce and rebuild the cauliflower shape, curved side up, on a round baking dish, inserting the peas and chick peas between the florets.

Pour any remaining sauce over and press the crushed cornflakes on to the cauliflower. Bake for 25–30 minutes until the cornflake coating is crisp.

Serve hot with *Baked Tomatoes* page 106 and *Low-fat Roast Potatoes* page 116.

TACOS MEXICANA

SERVES 4

An unopened carton of Taco shells will keep for months but once opened they go stale and soften. If you have a choice of sizes buy two small rather than one large. Fresh green chillies, after preparing, can be frozen blanched, when they will keep for three months.

8 Taco shells
2 tablespoons olive oil
1 large onion, finely chopped
1 medium green pepper, de-seeded and diced
2 green chillies, topped, de-seeded and finely sliced
25 g (1 oz) pine nuts, halved, or pumpkin seeds
salt
freshly ground black pepper

75 g (3 oz) Italian risotto rice
150 ml (¼ pint) tomato juice
600 ml (1 pint) hot stock
6–10 tablespoons cooked red kidney beans, crushed

Garnish ....
4 eggs, hard-boiled and chopped
75 g (3 oz) Edam cheese, diced
shredded lettuce

Place the Taco shells in a single layer on a baking tray. Set aside.

Heat the oil in a large frying-pan and cook the onion until soft. Add the diced pepper and sliced chillies and continue frying until the onions are brown and the peppers tender.

Stir in the pine nuts or pumpkin seeds, rice, tomato juice and stock. Cook gently for 25–35 minutes, stirring occasionally, until the liquid is absorbed and the rice is cooked. Taste and only season if needed with salt and pepper.

Stir in the kidney beans, remove from the heat and leave covered until required.

Pre-heat the oven to gas mark 4, 350°F (180°C).

Heat the Tacos in the oven for 2–3 minutes to crispen, then fill with the chilli mixture. Serve immediately with separate side dishes of the chopped egg and Edam, shredded lettuce and *Cucumber Raita* page 140.

VEGETABLE CURRY WITH BANANA SAMBAL

SERVES 4

This mild curry will please both first-time curry eaters and habitués. It comes from Pune, north of Bombay. Banana is an ideal accompaniment and will be soft when cooked.

25 g (1 oz) butter or margarine
2 medium onions, thinly sliced
2–4 tablespoons bottled mild curry
  paste (according to taste)
100 g (4 oz) carrots, sliced
1 large potato, peeled and cut into
  small chunks
600 ml (1 pint) hot stock
2 tablespoons desiccated coconut
1 tablespoon tomato purée
175 g (6 oz) cauliflower florets
100 g (4 oz) French beans, topped,
  tailed and halved

100 g (4 oz) cooked or frozen peas
salt
freshly ground black pepper

Garnish ....
3 green bananas
juice of half a lime
2 teaspoons ground cardamom
oil for frying
4 hard-boiled eggs, peeled and cut into
  6 wedges

Heat the butter or margarine in a large saucepan and fry the onion until golden. Stir in the curry paste and cook for 30 seconds.

Add the carrots and potato and sauté for 2 minutes, then pour in the stock, cover and simmer for 10 minutes until vegetables begin to soften.

Stir in the desiccated coconut, tomato purée, cauliflower and beans. Simmer for 10 minutes or until tender, then add the peas. Remove the lid and continue cooking until only a few tablespoons of liquid remain. Season with salt and pepper. Cover and keep warm.

Peel the bananas, cut into thick slices, brush with the lime juice and sprinkle with the cardamom. Heat a little oil in a pan and fry a few at a time until brown tinged. Drain briefly on kitchen paper.

Spoon the curried vegetables on to a heated serving platter and arrange the egg wedges and banana slices on top. Serve with special *Pilau Rice* page 120, *Cucumber Raita* page 140 and poppadums.

VEGGIE WEDGES

SERVES 4

This is probably a recipe that you will use again and again because it is easy, adaptable, quick to get ready and extremely economical. Dress it up with a luxury home-made sauce or cheat and use bottled spaghetti sauce.

450 g (1 lb) mixed cooked vegetables
  including onions (a frozen stew pack
  contains a suitable mixture)
3 tablespoons flour
2 tablespoons dried breadcrumbs
  (or crushed tea rusks)
1 egg

2 tablespoons bottled sauce
¼ teaspoon ground bay leaves
salt
freshly ground black pepper

extra dried breadcrumbs for coating
oil for shallow frying

Finely chop the vegetables and mix with the other ingredients (use a food processor if possible, adding the vegetables a few at a time before putting in the rest of the ingredients).

Taste and adjust the seasoning, then divide the mixture into eight and shape into wedges.

Press the dried crumbs on to all sides. Place in a single layer on a floured tray and refrigerate if time allows.

Heat about 2 cm (¾ in) oil in a frying-pan and fry the wedges for 5 minutes on each side or until golden and crisp.

Serve with a sauce of your choice (both *Quick Tomato Sauce* page 133 and *Espagnole Sauce* page 131 are good), with steamed cabbage and *Ratatouille* page 122.

WINTER VEGETABLE AND BARLEY HOT POT

SERVES 4

The porcini is a most sought after mushroom. Locating them is a favourite pastime for many an Italian who needs a licence to gather them from the woods. They can be eaten fresh but are more often sliced and dried in the sun. Very expensive to buy, specialist grocers in this country often stock them. They store well and only a few blades are required to give a real meaty taste to stews and casseroles. Substitutes give an inevitably poorer flavour but Shiitake mushrooms with their aromatic spicy flavour are acceptable.

2 tablespoons sunflower oil	4 dried porcini slices
4 medium onions, halved	1 tablespoon tomato purée
2 large carrots, thickly sliced	2 bay leaves
1 celery stick, sliced	150 ml (¼ pint) medium red wine
2 small turnips, peeled and diced	150 ml (¼ pint) stock
4 okra, rinsed, topped and tailed	salt
3 tablespoons pearl barley	freshly ground black pepper

Heat the oil in a large saucepan and gently fry the onions until golden. Add the carrots and celery, cook for a few minutes, then stir in the remaining ingredients, seasoning sparingly as the flavour will become more concentrated during lengthy cooking.

Bring to the boil, then reduce the heat as low as possible. Cover with a tight lid and cook gently for 2½ hours, checking occasionally to make sure it has not dried out. Add extra water as needed.

When the vegetables are tender and in a thick sauce, remove the bay leaves. Add 300 ml (½ pint) water, bring back to the boil, drop in uncooked *Sesame Seed Cheese Dumplings* page 155 and simmer covered for 20 minutes. Serve with broccoli florets cooked *al dente*.

WRAPPED CELERIAC PANCAKES

SERVES 4

This quite spectacular dish was served to me when I dined at Adlard's, a restaurant in Norwich. Julienne strips of peppers and carrot wrapped in what I imagined to be Chinese pancakes, but to my surprise the wrapper was made of paper-thin slices of celeriac. I have considerably modified David Adlard's recipe for the home cook. If you want to taste the enormously superior original, it will mean a trip to his excellent restaurant!

1 large fresh celeriac
1 egg yolk blended with 1 teaspoon
  arrowroot
¼ each of a yellow, green and red
  pepper
1 small carrot
1 teaspoon grated ginger root

garlic to taste, optional
salt
freshly ground black pepper
2 teaspoons olive oil

oil for shallow frying

Wash the celeriac and simmer whole in plenty of water until only tender enough for a knife to pierce the outer 2 cm (¾ in).

Cool, peel and cut at least 12 wafer thin slices from the thickest part. A food processor is not suitable as the slices must be large in diameter.

Slightly overlap and stick the edges of three slices together with the blended egg to form a triangle. Repeat with the remaining slices.

Cut the peppers and carrot into very thin strips and stir-fry with the ginger and garlic (if using) in the olive oil for 1–2 minutes. Drain thoroughly and season well.

Place some of the stir-fried vegetables on one edge of each triangle, roll over once, fold in the sides and then roll up to the top. Seal the edges with blended egg.

Fry, seam side down, in about 2.5 cm (1 in) of hot oil, turning the pancakes over when the underside is brown. Drain and serve immediately with *Red Pepper Compôte* page 123 and *Spicy Spinach* page 127.

Eggs and Cheese

AVOCADO AND PIMENTO OMELETTE

SERVES 2

However hard you try, it is almost impossible to prevent a peeled and cut avocado from discoloration. If you have to prepare ahead, sprinkle all avocado surfaces with fresh lemon juice and wrap tightly in freezer-quality cling film.

4 eggs	1 teaspoon fresh lemon juice
1 teaspoon milk	1 canned pimento, well drained
salt	butter or margarine
freshly ground black pepper	2 tablespoons chopped toasted
1 ripe avocado	sunflower seeds

Break 2 eggs each into two separate cups, adding half of the milk to each and seasoning with salt and pepper.

Halve the avocado and discard the stone. Peel with a stainless steel knife, cut into strips and sprinkle with the lemon juice. Slice the pimiento.

Set two dinner plates to heat.

Heat a small omelette pan, add a knob of butter or margarine, tipping the pan to coat evenly. When sizzling, pour in one cup of beaten egg mixture and lift the edges of the omelette to allow the uncooked mixture to run underneath.

Loosen from the pan with a palette knife and while still runny on top, arrange half the avocado and pimento on the section of the omelette furthest away from the pan handle. Flip the uncovered section over and cook for 15–20 seconds for the filling to heat. Slide the omelette on to a heated plate.

Cook the second omelette in the same way and sprinkle with sunflower seeds. Serve at once with *Duchesse Potatoes* page 110 and a watercress salad.

CIDER FONDUE

SERVES 2–3

A quick non-gooey family fondue that doesn't need special fondue equipment and that everyone can eat at the same time. However, if necessary the ever-supportive microwave will help to re-liquefy the mixture. If possible cook the fondue in a non-stick pan. The quantities in this recipe can be doubled without necessarily increasing the preparation times.

300 ml (½ pint) dry cider
225 g (8 oz) Lancashire cheese
25 g (1 oz) grated Gruyère cheese
1 tablespoon arrowroot
7 tablespoons whipping cream

¼ teaspoon mustard powder
⅛ teaspoon nutmeg
⅛ teaspoon white pepper
French bread, cut into bite-size
 chunks

Heat a serving bowl and keep hot.

Put the cider in a saucepan over the lowest possible heat and crumble in the Lancashire cheese. Add the Gruyère. Stir continuously until the cheeses have melted but have not completely merged with the cider.

Blend the arrowroot, cream and seasonings in a jug. Stir into the cider mixture until evenly blended and cook for 3–4 minutes stirring continuously until slightly thickened.

Pour into the pre-heated bowl and serve at once with a basket of French bread chunks for each person to spear with a fork and dunk into the fondue one piece at a time. Take care not to burn your mouth as the fork will be very hot.

Serve with sprigs of raw cauliflower, carrot and celery sticks and chicory leaves.

EGG, ONION AND TOMATO SKILLET

SERVES 4

Beef tomatoes can be anything from large to enormous and the flavour is unaffected by their size. Their firmness makes them ideal for use as culinary receptacles either for stuffings, macédoine salads or as in this recipe – nests.

1 tablespoon vegetable oil	freshly ground black pepper
2 large onions, finely sliced	4 eggs
2 beef tomatoes, halved crossways	4 tablespoons double cream.
salt	

Put the oil in a large non-stick frying-pan, spread the onions over the surface and cook over moderate heat for 10 minutes until they are tender.

Scoop the pulp from the tomatoes and add to the pan. Arrange the tomato shells cut side up on the onions. Season with salt and pepper.

Cover with a lid or buttered foil and cook until the tomato shells soften but still hold their shape.

Break the eggs into individual saucers and slide one into each tomato. Season lightly and spoon the cream over the yolks. Re-cover and cook for 4–5 minutes until the eggs are set to individual taste.

Serve at once on heated plates with freshly cooked leaf spinach and jacket potatoes.

ENCHILADAS SANTA FE

SERVES 4

This recipe makes unashamed use of such convenience foods as are available, nonetheless fresh chillis are preferable. If I were in a real hurry I would substitute a quarter teaspoon of chilli powder.

25 g (1 oz) butter or margarine
1 shallot, finely chopped
1–2 red chillis, halved, de-seeded
 and chopped
400 g (14 oz) can chopped tomatoes
 with herbs
½ teaspoon celery salt
freshly ground black pepper
2 eggs

300 ml (½ pint) Greek-style yogurt
150 ml (¼ pint) evaporated milk
4 *Flour Tortillas* page 152 or
 2 wholemeal pittas
175 g (6 oz) grated Edam, Gouda or
 similar cheese (sometimes obtainable
 ready grated)
small packet tortilla chips, crushed

Pre-heat the oven to gas mark 4, 350°F (180°C).

Melt the butter in a saucepan and sauté the shallot and chillis for 1–2 minutes. Stir in the tomatoes, celery salt and a generous shake of freshly ground black pepper. Cook for 5 minutes over moderate heat.

Meanwhile beat the eggs with half the yogurt and half the milk. Stir into the tomatoes and ignore any apparent curdling.

Mix the remaining yogurt with the milk, adjust the seasoning to taste and set aside.

Tear the flour tortillas or pitta in pieces, placing one layer in the base of an oven-proof dish. Cover with a layer of tomato sauce and some of the cheese. Repeat the layers finishing with the tortilla or pitta pieces. Pour over the reserved yogurt sauce to cover the dish and scatter with the crushed tortilla chips.

Bake for 25–35 minutes until the topping has set lightly and has browned.

Serve hot with sliced avocado dressed with *Warm Lemon Vinaigrette* page 136 and a plain green salad.

FARMHOUSE CHEDDAR AND WATERCRESS SOUFFLÉ

SERVES 4

Selecting Cheddar cheese from the ready-wrapped chill chest can be something of a minefield. Since this recipe consists largely of cheese, in order to get the best results it is wise to take advice from the sales assistant who will be able to suggest which is the strongest, most mature cheese. Packets of grated cheese often contain other ingredients. Beware!

50 g (2 oz) butter or margarine
45 g (1¾ oz) plain flour
300 ml (½ pint) milk
4 eggs, separated plus 2 egg whites
salt

freshly ground black pepper
175 g (6 oz) mature Cheddar
  cheese, grated
2 bunches watercress

Pre-heat the oven to gas mark 5, 375°F (190°C).

Butter an 18 cm (7 in) soufflé dish and refrigerate.

Melt the butter in a saucepan over moderate heat, stir in the flour and cook, stirring, for 1 minute. Remove from the heat and gradually add the milk, stirring until well blended. Return the pan to the heat and cook, stirring constantly until the sauce thickens.

Leave to cool for five minutes, then beat in the egg yolks. Season with salt and pepper and stir in the cheese.

Wash the watercress, thoroughly drain and pat in folded kitchen paper to dry thoroughly. Cut off the stalks and chop the leaves. Stir into the cheese mixture.

Whip the egg whites to soft peaks in a large bowl. Using a long handled metal spoon stir one-third into the cheese mixture, then fold in the remainder. Pour into the prepared dish, place on a baking tray and bake for 40–45 minutes until well risen and brown on top. Avoid opening the oven door during baking or the soufflé will collapse.

Serve immediately with *Low-Fat Roast Potatoes* page 116 and plain cooked carrot batons.

MOZZARELLA PIE

SERVES 4

There's mozzarella and mozzarella! The real Italian kind, which is packed with a certain amount of the whey, is softer. For this recipe the Danish or UK produced variety is admirable because it creates a more solid topping.

4 courgettes
1 large onion
1 stick celery
1 green pepper
1 small red pepper
salt

freshly ground black pepper
400 g (14 oz) can chopped tomatoes
 with herbs
225 g (8 oz) mozzarella cheese,
 thinly sliced

Pre-heat the oven to gas mark 4, 350°F (180°C).

Top, tail and slice the courgettes, thinly slice the onion and celery, and de-seed and thinly slice the peppers.

Butter a 1.2 litre (2 pint) pie dish and layer with the prepared vegetables, seasoning each with salt and pepper. Pour the tomatoes evenly on top. Cover with the mozzarella.

Bake for 35–45 minutes until the vegetables are tender and the topping nicely browned.

Serve with *Egg and Cucumber Salad* page 141 and *Garlic Bread Nuggets* page 153.

SUMMER EGGS IN RASPBERRY MAYONNAISE

SERVES 4–6

A complete main dish in itself but this cool salad can be served with accompanying salads to produce an even more substantial meal.

175 g (6 oz) long grain rice
1 tablespoon olive oil
1 teaspoon wine vinegar
salt
freshly ground black pepper
1 small red pepper, de-seeded
  and shredded

3 slender celery sticks, very
  finely sliced
6 eggs
50 g (2 oz) raspberries, sieved
  to remove the seeds
200 ml (7 fl oz) thick mayonnaise
10–12 tiny sprigs parsley

Cook the rice in plenty of boiling salted water until tender, about 10–15 minutes. Strain thoroughly in a colander and run through with cold water until the grains are all separated. Drain thoroughly.

Fork the oil and vinegar together and season with salt and pepper.

Plunge the red pepper shreds and celery slices into a pan of fast boiling water and cook for one minute, then strain immediately and cool under cold running water and drain thoroughly.

Mix the red pepper shreds and celery slices into the rice and moisten with the dressing. Spoon on to a serving platter.

Poach the eggs one at a time in a shallow pan of simmering salted water. When cooked, but not hard, remove from the pan and transfer carefully to a shallow dish and cover with cold water. When cool, lift the eggs out with a slotted spoon and arrange on the rice salad.

Beat the sieved raspberries into the mayonnaise. Coat the eggs with mayonnaise and garnish with parsley sprigs.

Serve with *Grated Carrot and Pineapple Salad* page 143 and *Hot Cheese Waffles* page 154.

TOMATO AND FRESH CORN SOUFFLÉ

SERVES 4

A textured soufflé with a pleasing golden hue. The corn kernels cook during baking. If you prefer a less crunchy texture, scrape the corn more finely. Kernels can be used if well-drained and crushed. The soufflé is baked at a fairly low temperature to avoid a crust setting before the mixture is well-risen.

2 corn cobs	175 ml (6 fl oz) tomato juice
40 g (1½ oz) butter or margarine	dash Worcestershire sauce or
2 spring onions, trimmed and	vegetarian equivalent
finely sliced	salt
40 g (1½ oz) plain flour	freshly ground black pepper
½ teaspoon mustard powder	4 large eggs, separated

Pre-heat the oven to gas mark 4, 350°F (180°C).

Butter an 18 cm (7 in) soufflé dish and refrigerate until needed.

Scrape the corn from the cobs and set aside.

Melt the butter in a saucepan over low heat and gently fry the onion for about two minutes until soft but not coloured. Stir in the flour and mustard powder and cook for 1 minute, then add the tomato juice and Worcestershire sauce and cook, stirring continuously until thick.

Place mixture in a large bowl, season with salt and pepper, leave for a few minutes to cool, then beat in the egg yolks and fold in the corn.

Beat the egg whites to soft peaks. Stir a quarter into the tomato mixture. Fold in the remainder with a large metal spoon. Pour into the prepared soufflé dish, smooth the top, place on a baking tray and bake immediately for 45–55 minutes until well risen and brown.

Serve immediately with *Watercress, Pear and Green Peppercorn Salad* page 151 and boiled new potatoes.

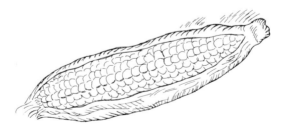

Pastry and Batter

ASPARAGUS FLAN

SERVES 4

Asparagus is a low-calorie vegetable with a regal flavour. The flan is filling and there will probably be enough for seconds or for serving the next day.

Pastry ....
225 g (8 oz) self-raising flour
100 g (4 oz) butter or hard margarine, diced
1 egg
1 tablespoon natural yogurt
2 pinches of salt

Filling ....
2 × 400 g (14 oz) cans asparagus spears

2 tablespoons natural yogurt
1 tablespoon cornflour
2 eggs, beaten
2 tablespoons grated Parmesan cheese
1 tablespoon grated Emmenthal cheese
salt
freshly ground black pepper
....
3 fresh asparagus spears, cooked

Pre-heat the oven to gas mark 6, 400°F (200°C).

Blend the pastry ingredients together in the food processor for 10–30 seconds until the dough gathers into a soft ball. Place in a plastic food bag and chill for 15 minutes or until the dough is firm enough to work.

Roll out and use to line a 25 cm (10 in) flan tin. Prick the base and sides with a fork. Put the flan dish on a baking tray and bake blind for 10–15 minutes until the pastry is crisp.

Meanwhile purée the entire contents of one can of asparagus with the yogurt, cornflour and eggs. Pour into a saucepan and cook over low heat, beating continuously until the sauce thickens. Stir in the cheeses and season to taste with salt and pepper.

Drain the asparagus from the second can and arrange as many of the spears as required in the pastry case. Cover with the sauce and garnish with the fresh asparagus spears, pressing them in slightly.

Reduce the oven temperature to gas mark 5, 375°F (190°C) and bake for 30–45 minutes until fairly firm and beginning to brown.

Serve hot with *Crispy Onion Rings* page 110 and *Minted Tomato Salad* page 147.

BRAZILIAN ROAST EN RÔBE

SERVES 4

Brazil nuts contain 66 per cent fat and 14 per cent protein. Chick peas are higher in protein but considerably lower in fat. With the carbohydrate in the flour and breadcrumbs this makes a well balanced meal but as the calorie count is high, small portions will suffice.

1 tablespoon olive oil
1 small onion, finely chopped
175 g (6 oz) chestnut or brown cap
 mushrooms, chopped
¼ stock cube, crumbled
175 g (6 oz) cooked chick peas,
 lightly crushed
50 g (2 oz) Brazil nuts, toasted
 and ground

100 g (4 oz) fresh granary loaf
 breadcrumbs
salt
freshly ground black pepper
2–3 small lemon balm leaves,
 finely scissored
250 g (9 oz) ready-to-roll
 shortcrust pastry

Pre-heat the oven to gas mark 6, 400°F (200°C).

Heat the oil in a large saucepan and gently fry the onion until soft. Stir in the mushrooms and continue frying until soft.

Add the stock cube and 5 tablespoons water. When dissolved mix in the chick peas, nuts and breadcrumbs. Taste before seasoning with salt and pepper, then add the lemon balm. The mixture should be soft. Add a little more water if needed.

Roll out three-quarters of the pastry and use to line a 450 g (1 lb) loaf tin. Line with foil to prevent the sides from collapsing and bake for 10 minutes only.

Roll out remaining pastry to form a lid and set aside.

Remove the foil, pack the filling into the pastry case, moisten the edges of the pastry lid and press on top. Slash through the pastry in three places to allow steam to escape.

Bake for 15 minutes, then reduce the heat to gas mark 3, 325°F (160°C) and bake for a further 20 minutes.

Remove carefully from the tin and serve sliced with *Caribbean Rice* page 108 and *Grilled Seasonal Vegetables* page 114.

BROCCOLI, ALMOND AND BAMBOO SHOOT CRISPY PANCAKES

SERVES 6

A more substantial main dish than you might think, these are truly delicious.

225 g (8 oz) broccoli florets
50 g (2 oz) flaked almonds, toasted
227 g (8 oz) can bamboo shoots,
  drained
6 tablespoons Greek-style yogurt
1 tablespoon Hoisin sauce
freshly ground black pepper

Batter ....
3 tablespoons plain flour
5 tablespoons milk
2 teaspoons soy sauce
5 large eggs
....
butter
vegetable oil

Crisp-cook the broccoli in a little boiling salted water. Drain and chop.

Coarsely chop the almonds and bamboo shoots. Mix in a bowl with the broccoli, yogurt, Hoisin sauce and black pepper to taste. Cover and keep warm.

Combine the flour, milk, soy sauce and eggs in a bowl and beat until smooth. Use this batter to make six 23 cm (9 in) pancakes, buttering the pan in between each. Transfer the pancakes to a plate, carefully placing them in a single layer on a sheet of non-stick parchment. They are delicate when hot but they firm up as they cool.

Spoon one-sixth of the vegetable mixture about 1 cm (½ in) from one edge of each pancake. Fold over once, tuck in both sides to seal, then roll up. Repeat to fill all the pancakes.

Prepare a hot grill. Remove the rack, lightly oil the grill pan and put in the pancake envelopes in a single layer seam side down. Brush the tops with oil, then cook until brown and crisp. Carefully turn the envelopes over to brown the other side.

Serve hot with *Rice and Mangetout Salad* page 148 and *Three–Lettuce Salad* page 150.

CELERY AND CASHEW NUT FILLED CHOUX

SERVES 4

Celery being a fresh flavoured vegetable, together with the crunchy nuts, makes an ideal filling, but crisp-cooked shredded onion and carrot are an alternative. Potato flour (fecule) is obtainable from health food stores. Instant potato powder could substitute.

175 ml (6 fl oz) milk
75 g (3 oz) butter
100 g (4 oz) plain flour, sifted
3 eggs, beaten
40 g (1½ oz) grated Cheddar cheese

Filling ....
225 g (8 oz) cooked celery, finely
  chopped
400 g (14 oz) fromage frais
2 tablespoons potato flour
50 g (2 oz) cashew nuts, toasted and
  coarsely chopped
salt
freshly ground black pepper

Put the milk and butter in a medium saucepan, heat until the butter is melted and the liquid rises rapidly up the sides of the pan. Immediately toss in the flour in one go. Switch off the heat and beat until the mixture forms a ball which leaves the side of the pan.

Transfer to a bowl and gradually beat in the egg until smooth. Blend in the cheese. Cover and leave until cold.

Pre-heat the oven to gas mark 7, 425°F (220°C).

Using 2 tablespoons, place four mounds of the paste well spaced out on a baking sheet lined with non-stick parchment. Place in the centre of the oven and bake for 12–15 minutes until brown.

Without opening the oven reduce the temperature to gas mark 5, 375°F (190°C) and bake for 10–15 minutes until the buns are doubled in size and crisp on the outside.

Meanwhile mix the filling ingredients together and season well. Heat, stirring continuously until thickened.

Split the choux in half and fill with the vegetable mixture, and serve with *Quick Tomato Sauce* page 133 or *Espagnole Sauce* page 131, baked marrow and purple sprouting broccoli.

CHINESE-STYLE STRUDEL

SERVES 4-6

Filo pastry is fun to work with and is obtainable from the freezer cabinets. The dimensions of the sheets vary according to the manufacturer and the method of packaging also varies so it is impossible to say how many sheets you will need, but certainly it will be less than one pack. To prevent drying out keep the delicate pastry covered, then butter, fill and roll up at one time. Hoisin and black bean sauce are stocked by major retailers.

175 g (6 oz) courgettes, diced
100 g (4 oz) cauliflower florets, diced
4 tablespoons bulgar (cracked wheat)
3 tablespoons cooked cut green beans
2 tablespoons sweetcorn kernels
2 tablespoons black bean sauce
1 tablespoon Hoisin sauce
pinch of cinnamon
salt
freshly ground black pepper
leaves of filo pastry, fresh or thawed
50-75 g (2-3 oz) butter or margarine,
    melted

Pre-heat the oven to gas mark 7, 425°F (220°C).

Cook the courgettes and cauliflower together in boiling salted water for 2 minutes. Strain liquid into a bowl and reserve. Refresh vegetables in a colander under cold running water, drain thoroughly and leave to cool.

Put the bulgar in a saucepan, add 8 tablespoons of the reserved liquid and heat gently until boiling. Cover and set aside until all the liquid is absorbed.

Mix in the courgettes, cauliflower, beans, sweetcorn, sauces and cinnamon, and season to taste.

Cut 12 pieces of filo each measuring approximately 16 cm × 28 cm (6½ in × 11 in). Lay one strip on top of another to make a double thickness and brush generously with the butter or margarine. Place some of the filling in a sausage shape along the short edges, leaving a 2 cm (¾ in) border at either side. Fold these sides over the filling and all the way up the filo sheet, brush them with more butter, roll up the strudels, then brush with the remaining butter.

Place on a buttered baking tray and bake for 10-15 minutes until pale golden and crisp.

Serve with *Garlic Sauté Mushrooms* page 113 and egg noodles.

CHOUX VEGETABLE BARS

SERVES 4–5

This recipe consists of a sandwich made from choux pastry filled with mixed vegetables in a thick white sauce flavoured with cheese. Use a packaged sauce or make it up in a saucepan or in the microwave, using 25 g (1 oz) butter or margarine, 25 g (1 oz) flour and 250 ml (8 fl oz) milk, salt and pepper. For speed substitute frozen mixed vegetables.

Pastry ....
50 g (2 oz) butter or margarine,
  at room temperature
200 g (7 oz) plain flour, sifted
5 eggs

Filling ....
150 ml (¼ pint) thick white sauce
350 g (12 oz) diced cooked mixed
  vegetables (e.g. peas, beans, carrots,
  leeks and cauliflower)

50 g (2 oz) grated hard cheese
  e.g. Parmesan or cheddar
salt
freshly ground black pepper
....
vegetable oil
about 100 g (4 oz) dried breadcrumbs

Pre-heat the oven to gas mark 7, 425°F (220°C).

Put 200 ml (7 fl oz) water and the butter in a medium saucepan. Bring slowly to the boil and when the water rises up the sides of the pan, tip in the flour all at once. Remove the pan from the heat and stir with a wooden spoon until the mixture forms a soft ball which comes away from the sides of the pan.

Leave for a few minutes, then beat in 3 of the eggs, one at a time. The mixture seems to curdle but soon blends to a smooth paste. Spoon on to a 23 cm × 33 cm (9 in × 13 in) baking tray lined with non-stick parchment and smooth evenly with a wet palette knife. Bake for 15–20 minutes until crisp on top.

Meanwhile mix the sauce with the vegetables and cheese, and season well.

Cut the pastry in half vertically, sandwich the halves with filling and cut the sandwich into 12 bars. Press well together. Dip the bars into the remaining beaten eggs, then coat with breadcrumbs and press in with a palette knife. Shallow or deep-fry, or bake in a hot oven in a few spoons of pre-heated oil. Serve with the reheated remaining vegetable mixture, *Creamed Spinach* page 109 and baby sweet corn.

CORNISH PASTIES

SERVES 4

A vegetarian equivalent of the more traditional Cornish pasty, but with a remarkably similar taste.

1 small potato
50 g (2 oz) swede
2 Brussels sprouts
175 g (6 oz) *Bolognese Lentil Mince*
  page 85
salt
freshly ground black pepper

250 g (9 oz) ready-to-roll
  shortcrust pastry

1 egg beaten with 1 tablespoon milk
  to glaze

Pre-heat the oven to gas mark 6, 400°F (200°C). Peel and dice the potato and swede, and coarsely chop the Brussels sprouts.

Cook the potato and swede in boiling salted water until just tender but not 'mashable'. Add the chopped sprouts and cook for 2 minutes. Drain, reserving 1–2 tablespoons of the liquid. Leave until cold.

Fold vegetables into the mince. Add sufficient of the reserved liquid to moisten and adjust the seasoning.

Divide the pastry into four equal parts and roll each out on a floured board to a 15 cm (6 in) circle. Use a small tea plate as a guide.

Place a quarter of the filling in the centre of each pastry circle, spreading it along slightly. Moisten the edges with the cooking liquid or cold water.

Lift up two opposite edges and press together above the filling. Flute the edges with finger and thumb and check that the pasties are sealed. Place on a buttered baking tray and brush with the beaten egg and milk.

Bake for 20–25 minutes until the pastry is set, browned and crisp. Remove from the baking tray with a fish slice and serve hot with *Cider Gravy* page 130, *Red Pepper Compôte* page 123 and *Petits Pois à la Française* page 118.

CRESPELLE RIPIENE

SERVES 4

An adaptation of a traditional Tuscan recipe, the original one using entirely fresh ingredients. It is made less laborious by substituting frozen spinach, canned tomatoes and a quick-cook sauce.

Batter ....
100 g (4 oz) plain flour
pinch of salt
2 eggs
250 ml (8 fl oz) skimmed milk
olive oil for frying

Sauce ....
75 g (3 oz) polyunsaturated margarine
75 g (3 oz) plain flour
750 ml (1¼ pints) skimmed milk
salt
freshly ground black pepper
5 tablespoons crushed canned
  tomatoes

Filling ....
175 g (6 oz) chopped cooked or frozen
  spinach, drained
300 g (11 oz) ricotta cheese, mashed
1 egg, beaten
½ teaspoon ground nutmeg
salt
freshly ground black pepper
....
3–4 tablespoons grated Parmesan
  cheese

Pre-heat the oven to gas mark 4, 350°F (180°C).

Prepare the pancake batter either in the blender or by hand and leave for 30 minutes.

Stir the batter, then make eight medium size pancakes, oiling the pan between each. Stack the pancakes between pieces of greaseproof paper and keep warm.

To make the sauce melt the margarine, in a saucepan, add the flour and milk and place over low heat, whisking continuously until the sauce bubbles and thickens.

Cook for a further two minutes. Season well and stir in the tomatoes. If added too soon the sauce will curdle.

Mix the filling ingredients, divide between the pancakes, roll up and place snugly in a single layer in a flameproof dish. Pour the sauce over the pancakes and sprinkle with the Parmesan.

Bake for 15–20 minutes, then place under a hot grill until bubbling and beginning to brown.

Serve with *Insalata Paese* page 145 and French beans.

DIJON TOMATO TARTE

SERVES 4

Select firm red tomatoes to set off the glamorous appearance of this essentially continental dish. The mustard makes it really exciting and is not excessive.

250 g (9 oz) ready-to-roll puff pastry flour
5 tablespoons Dijon mustard
175 g (6 oz) Gruyère cheese, thinly sliced
1 tablespoon horseradish sauce (do not use the creamed variety)

6–8 large tomatoes, skinned, quartered and de-seeded
2 tablespoons chopped fresh mixed herbs (chives, rosemary and sage)
freshly ground black pepper

Pre-heat the oven to gas mark 8, 450°F (230°C).

Roll out the pastry on a floured surface and use to line the base and sides of a 23 cm (9 in) buttered loose-bottomed flan tin.

Place the tin on a baking tray and prick the pastry with a fork. Spread the mustard over the base and sides and refrigerate for 15 minutes.

Arrange the Gruyère around the sides and base and sprinkle with the horseradish sauce. Cover with the tomato wedges curved sides upper-most. Speckle with herbs and plenty of black pepper.

Bake for 25–30 minutes or until the pastry is crisp. Check during the last 10 minutes of cooking and reduce the heat if necessary. It is important that the base is properly crispened.

Carefully remove the tart from the tin and ease on to a serving dish. Serve with *Lemon Cooked Celeriac* page 115 and *Peanut and Gem Lettuce Salad* page 147.

FRESH TOMATO AND OLIVE FLAN

SERVES 4

Primarily for summertime when tomatoes are cheapest, this can be adapted for use with the canned variety, but they must be strained until no further juice escapes or the mixture will be too slack to set properly. Save the juice to use in soups, casseroles or stock.

250 g (9 oz) ready-to-roll shortcrust
  pastry
6 tablespoons olive oil
1 small onion, chopped
1 kg (2 lb) firm ripe tomatoes,
  skinned, de-seeded and well drained
1 clove garlic, crushed
1 tablespoon chopped mixed fresh
  oregano and basil leaves
1 egg plus 3 egg yolks

3 tablespoons chopped fresh parsley
3 tablespoons tomato purée
12 stuffed green olives, chopped
1 teaspoon paprika
pinch of cayenne pepper
salt
freshly ground black pepper
12 stoned black olives
1 tablespoon grated Parmesan cheese

Pre-heat the oven to gas mark 6, 400°F (200°C).

Roll out the pastry to fit into a 23 cm (9 in) loose-bottomed flan tin. Prick thoroughly, chill for 15 minutes and bake blind for 15 minutes.

Heat 2 tablespoons oil in a saucepan and sauté the onion until soft. Add the tomatoes, garlic, oregano and basil, cover tightly with a lid and cook for 5 minutes over low heat. Raise the heat and cook uncovered until most of the liquid has evaporated, about 5 minutes.

Beat the eggs, parsley, tomato purée, green olives, paprika, cayenne, salt, pepper and 2 tablespoons oil in a mixing bowl and fold in the tomato mixture.

Spoon into the pastry case, smooth the top, decorate with the black olives and Parmesan, and drizzle over the last of the oil.

Put on a baking sheet, reduce to gas mark 5, 375°F (190°C) and bake for 25–30 minutes until set.

Serve with *Lemon Dressed Green Salad* page 146 and small jacket potatoes.

INDIVIDUAL RAISED PIES

SERVES 4

For a special occasion use the pastry to line a single, large, decorative sprung-type of pie mould and serve as a centre-piece.

Filling ....
1 small onion, finely chopped
1 small potato, peeled and diced
1 small carrot, finely diced
75 g (3 oz) cooked split peas, thick
1 tablespoon vegetable stock
2 sage leaves, finely chopped
salt
freshly ground black pepper

Pastry ....
285 g (10 oz) plain flour
½ teaspoon salt
100 g (4 oz) vegetable 'lard'
....
2–3 teaspoons agar-agar (for non-vegetarians) or 1 teaspoon gelatine
120 ml (4 fl oz) well-flavoured stock
beaten egg to glaze

Pre-heat the oven to gas mark 7, 425°F (220°C).

Mix all the filling ingredients together and set aside.

To make the pastry sift the flour and salt into a warm bowl. Heat the lard with 5 tablespoons water until melted, bring to the boil and immediately pour into the flour. Mix thoroughly with a wooden spoon. Knead until soft and pliable and divide the pastry into four, removing a quarter of each piece to use as a lid. Cover with a hot damp cloth or put in a polythene bag to prevent the pastry from cooling and cracking.

Flour the outside of a 5 cm (2 in) jar or smooth-sided ramekin. Working one at a time, shape the larger pieces of pastry into balls, then flatten with the palm of the hand. Ease each down the sides of the upturned jar. Reverse the jar on to a well greased baking tray and gently twist it out of the moulded pastry cases. Pack the cases with the filling.

Shape the lids, brush the edges with beaten egg and press on to the filling. Seal the edges by fluting with the finger and thumb.

Brush the pie tops with beaten egg and make a hole in the centre. Wrap a strip of greaseproof paper round the pies, securing with string.

Bake for 15 minutes, remove the strips and string, and brush the sides of the pies with beaten egg. Reduce the temperature to gas mark 4, 350°F (180°C) and bake for a further 25–30 minutes.

Dissolve the agar-agar or gelatine in the stock according to the packet and pour through the central hole into the pies. Leave to set.

Serve cold with *Curried Egg Salad* page 140 and *Avocado Salad* page 139.

NEEP BATTER PUDDING

SERVES 4

Four different root vegetables served in a crisp batter pudding case and coated with a simple parsley sauce so that the individual flavours can be identified. Root vegetables are sometimes mistakenly thought to taste the same but this recipe proves otherwise.

Batter ....
100 g (4 oz) plain flour
pinch of salt
1 egg
300 ml (½ pint) milk
2 tablespoons vegetable oil

Filling ....
1 small kohlrabi
2 small turnips
225 g (8 oz) parsnips
150 g (5 oz) carrots

Sauce ....
50 g (2 oz) soft margarine
50 g (2 oz) plain flour
600 ml (1 pint) milk
salt
freshly ground black pepper
4 tablespoons freshly chopped parsley
....
2 tablespoons salted peanuts, finely
  chopped

Beat the batter ingredients until smooth. Set aside for 30 minutes.

Pre-heat the oven to gas mark 7, 220°F (425°C).

Put a 23 cm × 28 cm (9 in × 11 in) oblong oven-proof dish on a baking tray, add the oil and heat in the oven for a few minutes until very hot. Stir the batter, pour into the dish and bake for 45 minutes until risen, crisp round the edges and set in the middle.

Meanwhile peel and dice the vegetables. Cook in boiling salted water until tender.

To make the sauce put the margarine, flour and milk in a saucepan and cook over moderate heat, stirring continuously until thickened. Season with salt and pepper, stir in the parsley and cook, still stirring for another 2 minutes.

Fill the pudding with the vegetables, mask them with the sauce and scatter the peanuts on top. Heat in the hot oven for 5 minutes.

Serve with any green leafy vegetable and *Paprika Potatoes* page 118.

ONION AND CHEDDAR QUICHES

SERVES 4

Individual flan tins are usually fluted and are about 10 cm (4 in) in diameter. They are worth buying if you enjoy presenting quiches in this appealing way. However, this recipe can be made into one large flan if you prefer. I give the recipe for shortcrust pastry but the shop-bought kind can be used as well.

Shortcrust Pastry ....
100 g (4 oz) plain flour
pinch of salt
50 g (2 oz) hard butter or margarine

Filling ....
25 g (1 oz) butter or margarine
1 Spanish onion, finely chopped

1 large egg
150 ml (¼ pint) single cream
salt
freshly ground black pepper
75 g (3 oz) grated Cheddar cheese
1 tablespoon chopped fresh parsley
cayenne pepper

To make the pastry sift the flour and salt into a bowl. Add the butter or margarine and chop with a knife until the mixture resembles bread-crumbs. Add 1½ tablespoons ice cold water. Mix with a fork until large lumps stick together. Gather into a ball with the finger tips, kneading only enough to achieve a smooth dough.

Lightly butter four individual 10 cm (4 in) flan dishes.

Pre-heat the oven to gas mark 6, 400°F (200°C).

Divide the pastry dough into four and roll each out to a 12.5 cm (5 in) round. Gently ease the pastry circles into the flan tins. Avoid stretching the pastry or it will shrink during baking. Without trimming, prick the sides and bases with a fork and chill for 15 minutes, then put a crumpled piece of foil in each tin, place on a baking sheet and bake for 15 minutes.

Meanwhile melt the butter or margarine in a frying-pan and sauté the onions until they are soft but not coloured. Drain on kitchen paper.

Beat the egg and cream together and season with salt and pepper.

Remove the foil from the pastry cases and sprinkle some of the cheese in the bottom. Cover with onion, then pour on most of the egg mixture, leaving a little to top up later. Reduce the temperature to gas mark 4, 350°F (180°C) and bake for 15–20 minutes until set.

Top up with egg, scatter with remaining cheese and bake for a further 5–6 minutes.

Garnish with the parsley and a shake of cayenne.

Serve hot with *Garlic and Fines Herbes Baked Mushrooms* page 112 and plain cooked carrots or cold with *Insalata Paese* page 145 and a green salad.

OYSTER MUSHROOM AND ASPARAGUS PIE

SERVES 4

Adapt this recipe for dinner parties if you wish by substituting fresh asparagus. It is easy and a microwave will make the job even easier.

225 g (8 oz) ready-to-roll puff pastry
1 × 340 g (12 oz) can cut asparagus
40 g (1½ oz) butter or margarine
40 g (1½ oz) plain flour
approx 450 ml (¾ pint) milk

salt
freshly ground black pepper
1 tablespoon olive oil
100 g (4 oz) oyster mushrooms

Pre-heat the oven to gas mark 8, 450°F (230°C).

Roll out the pastry to a 28 cm (11 in) circle and fit into a buttered or non-stick pie plate. Prick well with a fork and freeze until hard.

Strain the asparagus and measure the liquid. Make up to 600 ml (1 pint) with milk.

Melt the butter in a saucepan, stir in the flour and cook over moderate heat for 1 minute. Gradually add the asparagus liquid and cook until thickened, stirring all the time. Season with salt and pepper. Mix in the asparagus, cover and set aside.

Bake pastry for 25 minutes, then quickly press down the risen centre with a large spoon and continue baking for 10 minutes or until the centre re-puffs. Reduce to gas mark 5, 375°F (190°C) and continue baking for 10 minutes. Switch off and leave to cool slowly in the oven.

Leaving a 2.5 cm (1 in) border, cut out the centre pastry to form a lid. Remove some of the softer inside pastry layers to leave a well. Reheat the pastry in a hot oven for a few minutes and at the same time reheat the asparagus mixture.

Heat the oil in a frying-pan and sauté the mushrooms for 3–4 minutes.

Pour the filling into the pastry case and arrange the drained mushrooms on top. Half cover with the reserved pastry lid and serve with *Rice and Lentil Compôte* page 124 and crisp-cooked Kenyan green beans.

ROQUEFORT AND BROCCOLI QUICHE

SERVES 4

A creamy quiche with quite a bite which, when baked in a loose-bottomed, fluted flan tin, is so reminiscent of local French cuisine. Roquefort is made from ewe's milk and is one of the most expensive of the French cheeses but there is no rind which means no waste.

Pastry ....
175 g (6 oz) plain wholemeal flour
¼ teaspoon cayenne pepper
75 g (3 oz) chilled unsalted butter, diced
....
hazelnut oil

Filling ....
2 shallots, finely chopped
275 g (10 oz) broccoli florets
4 eggs
175 g (6 oz) can unsweetened evaporated milk
freshly ground black pepper
100 g (4 oz) Roquefort cheese, coarsely chopped

Pre-heat the oven to gas mark 6, 400°F (200°C).

To make the pastry sift the flour and cayenne together through a coarse sieve and rub in the butter until the mixture resembles bread crumbs. Add sufficient ice cold water (about 5–6 tablespoons) to mix to a firm dough. Wholemeal flour absorbs more water than white flour.

Roll out the dough and fit into a loose-bottomed 20 cm (8 in) flan tin rubbed with hazelnut oil. Chill for 20 minutes.

To prepare the filling, cook the shallots and broccoli in a minimum of boiling salted water until tender. Strain, reserving the liquid. Chop vegetables finely.

Beat the eggs with the milk, 4 tablespoons of the reserved liquid and a generous shake of pepper.

Scatter the cheese in the pastry case, cover with the broccoli mixture and strain over the beaten egg liquid.

Bake for 35–45 minutes until puffed up and golden brown. No liquid should show when a table knife is inserted in the filling.

Serve hot with steamed carrots and *Caramel Glazed Baby Onions* page 108.

SAMOSAS

SERVES 4

Samosas are little triangular pastries filled with curry flavoured vegetables. Although less tasty, 1 tablespoon of garam masala can be used in place of the individual spices.

2 tablespoons vegetable oil
1 small onion, very finely chopped
¼ teaspoon garlic paste
½ teaspoon each of ground
  cardamom, cumin, turmeric and
  cayenne pepper
1 teaspoon ground coriander
⅛ teaspoon each of ground ginger

and ground fenugreek
¼ teaspoon salt
1 small potato, cooked and diced
150 g (5 oz) mixed vegetables,
  cooked and diced
8–10 sheets of filo pastry
melted butter or margarine

Pre-heat the oven to gas mark 7, 425°F (220°C).

Heat the oil and fry the onion until soft. Add the garlic paste, spices and salt and cook for 30 seconds, stirring all the time.

Add 1 tablespoon water, the potato and the other vegetables, mixing them until they bind together.

Cut the filo pastry into four strips approximately 9 cm × 35 cm (3½ in × 14 in). Brush generously with melted butter or margarine.

Place a spoonful of filling on one corner of each strip and fold over, down, sideways and down, repeating all the way to the bottom of the strip to form triangular parcels and making about seven folds in all.

Place on a buttered baking sheet and bake for 10 minutes or until the pastry is brown and crisp.

Serve as part of a 'Curry Dinner' with *Cauliflower and Potato Bhajis* page 19 and *Dhal* page 88.

SAVOURY ROLY POLY

SERVES 4–6

Steam or bake this savoury pudding and vary the filling according to the ingredients at hand. The sole consideration is that the filling must not be too wet or the inside of the pastry will be soggy.

Filling ....
350 g (12 oz) mixed diced cooked
  vegetables
2 tablespoons oat bran
4 tablespoons mayonnaise
1 tablespoon bottled tomato sauce
2 tablespoons milk
salt
freshly ground black pepper

Pastry ....
225 g (8 oz) plain flour
3 teaspoons baking powder
1 teaspoon salt
100 g (4 oz) vegetable suet
2 tablespoons chopped fresh parsley

First mix all the filling ingredients together and set aside.

To make the pastry sieve the flour, baking powder and salt into a mixing bowl. Stir in the suet and the parsley, then add 175 ml (6 fl oz) cold water in one go and mix to a soft dough. Add extra water only if necessary.

Knead lightly, then gently roll out on a floured board to a 23 cm × 25 cm (9 in × 10 in) rectangle. Dampen the surface and spread with the filling, leaving a 2 cm (¾ in) border.

Without using undue pressure, roll up Swiss roll fashion from one long edge to completely enclose the filling. Press the edges to seal. Wrap in buttered greaseproof paper and overwrap with a large piece of foil. Twist the ends to completely secure.

Cook in a steamer or steam on a rack over boiling water for 2–2½ hours in a tightly lidded pan, topping up with boiling water when necessary. The water must not come into direct contact with the pudding. OR: Bake in a pre-heated oven at gas mark 5, 375°F (190°C) for 45–50 minutes, opening the wrapping for the final 15 minutes to brown the top.

Serve sliced, coated with *Sage and Onion Sauce* page 133, *Baked Tomatoes* page 106 and spring greens.

71

SLATTED PASTIES WITH LEEK PURÉE

SERVES 4

The inspiration for this recipe was the Eccles cake! It is helpful if using frozen pastry to allow it to thaw out completely at room temperature. When fairly soft it is easier to gather up the edges. Chilling the pasties before baking should remedy any damage caused by over-softening.

1 small parsnip	1 teaspoon Worcestershire sauce
1 small potato	or vegetarian equivalent
4 cauliflower florets, separated	salt
into tiny sprigs	freshly ground black pepper
25 g (1 oz) butter or margarine	450 g (1 lb) ready-to-roll puff pastry
1 small onion, chopped	1 egg, beaten
175 g (6 oz) continental lentils,	450 g (1 lb) leeks, sliced
cooked or canned	4 tablespoons single cream

Cook the parsnip and potato in boiling salted water, add the cauliflower towards the end of cooking and cook for 2 minutes until just tender. Drain and dice the vegetables.

Melt the butter or margarine in a saucepan, add the onion and cook until just turning colour. Fold in the parsnip, potato, cauliflower, lentils and Worcestershire sauce, season with salt and pepper and leave to cool.

Pre-heat the oven to gas mark 8, 450°F (230°C).

Roll out the pastry on a floured surface to a thickness of 1 mm (less than ⅛ in). Cut out 8 × 15 cm (6 in) saucer-sized pieces.

Place a dessertspoonful of the filling in the centre of each, damp the border of the pastry and gather up the edges, pinching them together above the filling to enclose completely. Turn the pasties over and press lightly to flatten to 1 cm (½ in) thick. Slit through the top of the pastry in three places with kitchen scissors. Brush with the beaten egg, place on a buttered baking tray and chill for 15–30 minutes.

Meanwhile put the sliced leeks in a saucepan with salt and freshly ground black pepper and barely cover with water. Cover tightly with a lid and simmer until tender. Purée in the food processor, add the cream and mix briefly. Return to the saucepan and reheat just before serving.

Bake the pasties for 15–20 minutes until puffed up and golden brown. Serve hot, spooning the leek purée around the pasties, together with *Savoy Cabbage and Tomato Fricassée* page 126 and *Baked Piperade* page 105.

SPINACH CORACLES

SERVES 4

These crisp batter puddings can be baked equally well and more quickly in small bun tins or in a single large round shallow cake tin which will take about 35 minutes. The freshly cooked filling with its bright true colour should be spooned on to the puddings and garnished with toasted almond flakes just before serving, to prevent them going soggy.

Vegetable oil for the tins

Batter ....
150 g (5 oz) wholemeal flour
2 eggs
300 ml (½ pint) milk
pinch salt

Filling ....
75 g (3 oz) butter or polyunsaturated
  margarine

75 g (3 oz) plain white flour
450 ml (¾ pint) milk
750 g (1½ lb) frozen or cooked
  chopped spinach
3 tablespoons chopped chives
6 rounded tablespoons frozen peas
salt
freshly ground black pepper
25 g (1 oz) flaked almonds, toasted

Pre-heat the oven to gas mark 7, 425°F (220°C).

Generously oil 8 individual (preferably non-stick) 7.5 cm (3 in) tins. Put the tins on a baking tray and heat in the oven for 3–4 minutes or until the oil sizzles.

Sift the wholemeal flour into a mixing bowl and set aside the residual bran. Beat the eggs, milk and salt together, pour into the flour and beat to a smooth batter, adding 2 tablespoons cold water. One-third fill heated tins with batter and bake for about 15–20 minutes until well risen and brown around the edges.

While baking make a white sauce. Melt the butter or margarine, stir in the white flour and gradually add the milk. Stir in the spinach, chives, peas and half the reserved bran (use the remainder for other recipes). Cook gently, stirring continuously for 3–4 minutes. Season to taste.

Unmould the puddings, top with the filling and garnish with the almonds. Serve at once with plain cooked sliced carrots and grilled tomatoes dusted with a little grated nutmeg.

SPINAKOPITA

SERVES 6

Spinakopita is a delectable Greek dish. I have added a few extra ingredients to further improve its nutritional value. A small portion goes quite a long way and it can be eaten hot or cold.

450 g (1 lb) fresh spinach
100 g (4 oz) butter or margarine
175 g (6 oz) courgettes, topped,
  tailed and thinly sliced
2 shallots, finely chopped
40 g (1½ oz) pine nuts, coarsely
  chopped

6 black olives, stoned and sliced
175 g (6 oz) Feta cheese, crumbled
2 eggs beaten
freshly ground black pepper
1 teaspoon olive oil
8 sheets of filo pastry

Pre-heat the oven to gas mark 4, 350°F (180°C).

Remove the tough stalks from the washed spinach, shred the leaves and dry thoroughly to remove all excess moisture.

Melt 15 g (½ oz) of the butter in a large saucepan and sauté the courgettes for 3 minutes until tender. Add the spinach and shallots and stir for 1 minute.

Remove the pan from the heat and stir in the pine nuts, olives and Feta cheese. Mix in the beaten egg and season with pepper.

Melt the remaining butter or margarine and olive oil and brush over the base and sides of a deep baking tin approximately 20 cm × 28 cm (8 in × 11 in).

Line with two sheets of filo pastry, brushing the top with butter or margarine. Cover with two more filo sheets, buttering as before. Spread evenly with the filling.

Cover with the remaining filo, brushing sheets with butter or margarine. Fold the edges of the pastry down to seal and pour over any remaining butter or margarine.

Score the top layers with a sharp knife and bake in the centre of the oven for 30–40 minutes until golden brown and crisp on top.

Serve with *Minted Tomato Salad* page 147 and *Petits Pois à la Française* page 118.

VOL AU VENT SELECTION

SERVES 4

Make your own vol au vent cases from home-made puff pastry, otherwise make use of the splendid frozen ones from the freezer cabinet. So long as the proportion of sauce to filling ingredient is maintained, the selection of filling can be varied according to taste.

16 ready-to-bake 5 cm (2 in) diameter vol au vent cases

Sauce ....
15 g (½ oz) polyunsaturated margarine
15 g (½ oz) plain flour
6 tablespoons milk
salt
freshly ground black pepper

Mushroom filling ....
6–8 button mushrooms, finely chopped
1 tablespoon freshly chopped chives

Egg filling ....
1 hard boiled egg chopped
pinch of curry powder

Cheese filling ....
1 tomato, skinned and chopped
2 tablespoons grated mature Cheddar cheese
⅛ teaspoon mustard powder

Chick pea filling ....
1 tablespoon chopped cooked chick peas
1 teaspoon Tahini
....
polyunsaturated margarine

Pre-heat the oven to gas mark 8, 450°F (230°C).

Place the vol au vent cases on a buttered baking sheet and bake for 10–12 minutes until well risen and pale brown. Remove from the oven but do not switch off.

While the pastry is baking, blend the sauce ingredients in a saucepan. Cook over moderate heat, whisking continuously until thick. Season with salt and pepper.

Divide the sauce between the fillings. Fill the vol au vent cases with each of the four fillings (four cases per filling) and top with tiny dabs of butter. Return to the oven for 2–3 minutes to heat through.

Serve with *Toujours Cauliflower* page 129 and *Saffron Rice* page 126.

Pasta and Rice

ALMOND AND MACARONI LAYER

SERVES 4

A simple everyday meal containing all the basic nutrients. The sauces can be prepared ahead, making the dish even quicker to create.

50 g (2 oz) butter or margarine
50 g (2 oz) plain flour
600 ml (1 pint) milk
225 g (8 oz) chopped frozen or
  cooked spinach
pinch nutmeg
227 g (8 oz) can chopped tomatoes

½ stock cube
salt
freshly ground black pepper
175 g (6 oz) macaroni
2 large carrots, sliced and boiled
  until tender
40 g (1½ oz) flaked almonds, toasted

Pre-heat the oven to gas mark 6, 400°F (200°C).

Melt the butter or margarine in a medium saucepan and stir in the flour. Cook over low heat for 1 minute, stirring continuously, then add the milk and continue cooking still stirring until thick.

Pour half of the sauce into another pan. Add the spinach and nutmeg to one and the tomatoes and stock cube to the other.

Heat both pans until the spinach, if frozen, has thawed and the sauce is blended to a purée. Stir the tomato mixture until the stock cube has dissolved and the sauce is even. Season both sauces with salt and pepper.

Cook the macaroni in a pan of boiling salted water until tender. Cooking time depends on the type of macaroni you are using.

Butter a shallow ovenproof dish and pour in the tomato mixture. Cover with the macaroni and a layer of carrots.

Pour the spinach sauce evenly on top. Cover with a lid and bake for 15 minutes.

Remove the lid and garnish with the toasted almond flakes. Serve with a mixed green salad only, as a second vegetable would be excessive.

GREEN CANNELLONI WITH RICOTTA FILLING

SERVES 4

Home-made pasta can be time consuming to make but really does taste good. Sometimes it is possible to buy fresh lasagne which can be used in this recipe. Dried uncoloured cannelloni tubes have a completely different texture.

Pasta	Filling
275 g (10 oz) plain flour	275 g (10 oz) ricotta cheese
1 teaspoon salt	2 tablespoons chopped fresh parsley
15 g (½ oz) soft margarine	salt
2 eggs	freshly ground black pepper
50 g (2 oz) cooked chopped spinach, pressed until dry	2 tablespoons grated Parmesan cheese
	Quick Tomato Sauce page 133 with 2 teaspoons added chopped basil

Pre-heat the oven to gas mark 6, 400°F (200°C).

To make the pasta put the flour, salt, margarine, eggs and spinach into the food processor with 1 tablespoon of lukewarm water. Process for 10–15 seconds. The dough should be soft and manageable. If it seems too heavy add a little more water and mix briefly.

Turn on to a floured surface and roll out thinly to a thickness of 2 mm (less than ⅛ in). Cut into twelve 12.5 cm × 7.5 cm (5 in × 3 in) rectangles. Cover with a cloth while preparing the filling.

Mix all the filling ingredients to a paste and adjust the seasoning.

Place a 'sausage' of filling along one long edge of each pasta piece, leaving a 1 cm (½ in) border at either end. Roll up from the filled edges and place the cannelloni side by side in a single layer in a buttered shallow dish.

Pour over the sauce, cover with buttered foil and bake for 20–25 minutes until bubbling hot.

Serve three per person with mangetout and *Caramel Glazed Baby Onions* page 108.

FARFALLE WITH WALNUT AND PUMPKIN SEED SAUCE

SERVES 4

Little pasta bows mixed with butter beans and spring onions, and a light coating of creamy sauce. Pasta bows retain their shape and left-overs can be gently reheated in the microwave.

Sauce ....

2 egg yolks
2 teaspoons bottled English mustard
1 teaspoon fresh lemon juice
salt
freshly ground black pepper
6 tablespoons walnut oil
2 tablespoons pumpkin seeds, toasted
  and lightly crushed

....

8 thick spring onions, trimmed and
  sliced diagonally
225 g (8 oz) farfalle
150 g (5 oz) butter beans, halved
few sprigs parsley

To make the sauce whisk the egg yolks for one minute in a small bowl. Beat in the mustard, lemon juice, salt and pepper. When well mixed, whisk in the olive oil drop by drop until emulsified. Adjust the seasoning. Stir in the pumpkin seeds.

Cook the spring onions in a large pan of boiling salted water until crisp-cooked, then add the farfalle and boil rapidly for 5 minutes until half-cooked, add the butter beans and continue cooking for about 5 minutes until the pasta is just tender.

Drain thoroughly, then turn into a heated serving dish. Quickly beat up the sauce, pour over the pasta and mix to coat.

Garnish with the parsley and serve immediately with *Grilled Seasonal Vegetables* page 114 and a mixed salad if desired.

ROAST PUMPKIN SEED AND RICE TOMATOES

SERVES 4

Pumpkin seeds are hidden inside the pods found inside the pumpkin. It is a tedious job to shell the seeds and not very costly to buy them ready podded in health food shops and some supermarkets. Roast them under the grill, in the conventional or microwave oven. They pop while browning and should be stirred frequently.

4 beef tomatoes
15 g (½ oz) butter or margarine
1 slender leek, white part only,
  chopped
100 g (4 oz) cooked brown rice
1 broccoli floret, chopped
50 g (2 oz) sweetcorn kernels

1 tablespoon roasted pumpkin seeds,
  chopped
¼ teaspoon Worcestershire sauce or
  vegetarian equivalent
salt
freshly ground black pepper
50 g (2 oz) Mozzarella cheese, diced

Pre-heat the oven to gas mark 6, 400°F (200°C).

Remove a lid from the rounded ends of the tomatoes. Scoop out the seeds and pulp, chop the lids and save to use in another recipe.

Put the butter or margarine and the leek in a saucepan and cook over low heat until the leek softens.

Mix in the rice, broccoli, sweet corn, pumpkin seeds, Worcestershire sauce and season to taste with salt and pepper. Stuff the mixture into the tomato shells and place in a single layer in a buttered dish. Top with the Mozzarella. Pour 3–4 tablespoons of water around the tomatoes.

Bake for 20 minutes until the tomato shells soften slightly and the cheese begins to brown.

Serve with *Swede and Carrot Purée* page 128 and *Tricorn Puffs* page 156.

SAUTERNE MUSHROOMS WITH CRISP VERMICELLI

SERVES 4

This recipe is an adaptation of another of chef David Adlard's recipes – assorted mushrooms and artichokes in a creamy sauce sandwiched between disks of crisp vermicelli. The sauce is less rich and possibly less magnificent, but healthier, when yogurt replaces the cream. To make pasta blend 250 g (9 oz) fine semolina, a pinch of salt, 2 eggs and one extra yolk in the food processor, leave for 30 minutes, pass through a pasta machine or cut into thin strips. Leave to dry. I used vermicelli nests from a packet.

200 g (7 oz) vermicelli
sunflower oil
550 g (1¼ lb) assorted oyster,
  chestnut and button mushrooms
1 shallot, chopped
4 artichoke hearts, sliced
salt
freshly ground black pepper

200 ml (7 fl oz) Sauterne wine
⅛ teaspoon rosemary leaves,
  finely scissored
2 tablespoons Madeira
3 tablespoons double cream or
  Greek-style yogurt
1 teaspoon cornflour

Cook the vermicelli in plenty of boiling salted water according to the instructions on the packet, drain, then toss in 1 tablespoon of oil to keep the strands separate.

Half-fill an upturned 7.5 cm (3 in) metal pastry cutter with vermicelli. Heat 3–4 tablespoons of oil in a large frying-pan and using a fish slice, place both pasta and cutter in the hot oil. Cook for a few seconds, then remove the cutter with tongs, carefully refill with pasta and repeat the process with the remainder. Turn the pasta discs over as soon as golden underneath. Drain and keep warm.

Slice, then stir-fry the mushrooms and shallot in 2 tablespoons oil, about 2–3 minutes. Add the artichokes and season well.

In a small pan simmer the wine and rosemary until reduced by half, remove from the heat, add the Madeira and the cream or yogurt blended with the cornflour. Pour into the mushrooms and heat, stirring continuously, until bubbling. Sandwich the vermicelli with the mushrooms, spooning the surplus on the side of the plate.

Serve with plain cooked shredded kale and baby sweet corn.

Previous page **Roquefort and Broccoli Quiche (page 69) with Caramel Glazed Baby Onions (page 108)**

Left **French Bean, Cauliflower and Red Pepper Roulade (page 24)**
Right **Green Cannelloni with Ricotta Filling (page 77)**

Left **Crown of Vegetables with Mushroom Filling (page 22)**
Right **Norfolk Kebabs (page 98) with Roast Pumpkin Seed and Rice Tomatoes (page 79)**

Left **Crespelle Ripiene
(page 62) with Insalata
Paese (page 145)**
Right **Orange Flavoured
Stuffed Marrow
(page 33) with Quick
Tomato Sauce (page 133)
and Paprika Potatoes
(page 118)**

Overleaf **Cauliflower and
Potato Bhajis (page 19)
with Samosas (page 70)
and Dhal (page 88)**

SPAGHETTI WITH TOMATO AND MUSHROOM SAUCE

SERVES 4

Allow about 75 g (3 oz) spaghetti per person. Anyone bad at guessing can buy a spaghetti measure which has varying sized measuring holes. The wine makes a big difference so be sure it is a drinkable one!

olive oil
1 medium onion, chopped
1 clove garlic, crushed or a 5 mm
  (¼ in) squeeze garlic paste
225 g (8 oz) small mushrooms,
  quartered
400 g (14 oz) can chopped tomatoes
2 tablespoons tomato purée

about 10 fresh basil leaves, scissored
75 g (3 oz) freshly grated Parmesan
  cheese
freshly ground black pepper
12–15 tablespoons medium red wine
salt
350 g (12 oz) spaghetti

Heat about 2 tablespoons olive oil in a large frying-pan and cook the onions and garlic until golden. Stir in the mushrooms, tomatoes, tomato purée, basil leaves and a third of the Parmesan, adding pepper generously to taste.

Bring to the boil then, without covering, simmer until reduced to a thick consistency. Add the wine and an equal quantity of water, cover with a lid and continue cooking over the lowest possible heat for 20–25 minutes.

Cook the spaghetti so that it is ready at the same time as the sauce. Bring a large pan of water to the boil adding 2 teaspoons salt to every litre (1¾ pints) water. Add a teaspoon of oil. Immerse the spaghetti, stirring frequently with a fork to prevent bunching. Do not cover the pan. As soon as a strand can be easily broken with the side of a fork, remove the pan from the heat and drain through a lightly oiled colander.

Turn into a heated serving dish and pour over the sauce. Sprinkle the rest of the Parmesan over the individual servings.

Serve with Brussels sprouts and *Medley of Green Beans* page 117.

WILD RICE AND MUSHROOM PUFF

SERVES 4

Wild rice is not strictly speaking rice and can be categorised as a grass. The grains are black and spiky but when cooked split open and are flaked with white, and have a nutty flavour. If preferred, divide the mixture and cook in separate dishes and reduce the cooking time by about two-thirds.

75 g (3 oz) wild rice, rinsed and drained
salt
40 g (1½ oz) butter or margarine
40 g (1½ oz) plain flour

275 ml (9 fl oz) hot stock
4 eggs
freshly ground black pepper
100 g (4 oz) cooked or canned chopped mushrooms

Put the rice, ½ teaspoon salt and about 450 ml (¾ pint) water in a saucepan. Bring to the boil, then reduce the heat, cover and simmer for 45–50 minutes until the grains puff open. Drain.

Pre-heat the oven to gas mark 4, 350°F (180°C).

Melt the butter or margarine in a saucepan over moderate heat and blend in the flour. Cook, stirring for one minute, then add the stock and continue cooking, still stirring until the sauce thickens. Remove from the heat and pour into a bowl to cool slightly.

Whisk the eggs until frothy, add to the sauce, season with pepper, adding salt sparingly. Whisk thoroughly. Fold in the mushrooms and the wild rice.

Pour into a large oval buttered pie dish and bake for 30–40 minutes until puffed up and just firm on top. Serve at once with grilled halved beef tomatoes topped with chopped chives and *Braised Celery* page 106.

Pulses and Beans

ARTICHOKE AND BROWN LENTIL LASAGNE

SERVES 6

Brown lentils, sometimes labelled Chinese lentils, are a grey-brown colour and larger than a red split lentil. Their rich meaty flavour makes them an excellent substitute for the minced beef used in an authentic Lasagne al Forno.

3 tablespoons olive oil
1 medium onion, finely chopped
1 clove garlic, crushed
1 medium carrot, finely chopped
175 g (6 oz) small mushrooms, sliced
350 g (12 oz) brown lentils, rinsed
  and boiled rapidly for 10 minutes
227 g (8 oz) can tomatoes
1 tablespoon tomato purée
150 ml (¼ pint) red wine
3 bay leaves
salt

freshly ground black pepper
900 ml (1½ pints) milk
100 g (4 oz) polyunsaturated
  margarine or soft butter
75 g (3 oz) plain flour
generous pinch of nutmeg
8 artichoke bottoms, cooked or
  canned, sliced
12 sheets pre-cooked lasagne leaves
2–3 tablespoons freshly grated
  Parmesan cheese (optional)

Heat the oil and fry the onion, garlic and carrot until soft. Stir in the mushrooms, drained lentils, tomatoes and their juice, tomato purée, wine and 600 ml (1 pint) boiling water and bay leaves. Cover and simmer for 35–40 minutes until the lentils are tender. Remove the bay leaves. Season with salt and pepper, adding extra water if necessary.

Meanwhile put the milk, margarine or butter and flour in a saucepan. Whisk over low heat until the sauce thickens. Season with salt, pepper and nutmeg.

Butter a large shallow dish. Starting with a layer of lentils and artichokes, cover with a layer of white sauce and pasta and repeat, using up all ingredients and ending with white sauce.

Sprinkle evenly with Parmesan. Cover the dish with buttered foil and bake for 30 minutes at gas mark 5, 375°F (190°C). Uncover, raise the heat to gas mark 7, 425°F (220°C). Return to the oven for 10 minutes or until browned and bubbling.

Serve with *Petits Pois with Cashew Nuts* page 119 and *Pink Grapefruit and Watercress Salad* page 148.

AUBERGINE TOMATO AND BEAN CASSEROLE

SERVES 4

Cook raw blackeye beans in four times their dry volume of water. Add a teaspoon of vegetable oil to the pot to reduce foaming. Fast boil for 10 minutes, then reduce the heat and simmer covered until they are tender. A 400 g (14 oz) can of beans should produce the required amount of drained beans.

1–2 aubergines, total weight 450 g (1 lb)
1 onion, chopped
75 g (3 oz) butter or margarine
1 tablespoon vegetable oil
225 g (8 oz) cooked blackeye beans.
450 g (1 lb) tomatoes, skinned and sliced

2 tablespoons chopped fresh parsley
½ teaspoon freshly ground black pepper
150 ml (¼ pint) well-flavoured stock
salt
8 tablespoons fresh white breadcrumbs

Pre-heat the oven to gas mark 4, 350°F (180°C).

Cube the aubergine and lightly fry with the onion in 50 g (2 oz) of the butter or margarine and the oil until lightly browned. Switch off the heat but leave the pan on the cooker.

Remove the aubergine and onion from the pan with a slotted spoon and layer in a casserole dish with the beans, tomatoes and three-quarters of the parsley.

Stir the pepper into the stock, seasoning with salt if needed. Pour the stock over the vegetables and bake for 25 minutes.

Meanwhile add the remaining butter to the frying pan and fry the breadcrumbs until golden. Spoon over the vegetables and continue baking for a further 10 minutes.

Sprinkle with remaining parsley. Serve hot with *Paprika Potatoes* page 118 and spring greens.

BOLOGNESE LENTIL MINCE

SERVES 4

Just as good as mince but with far less fat and cholesterol free. Use this recipe in place of any requiring mince.

2 tablespoons vegetable oil
1 large onion, chopped
1 medium carrot, finely chopped
½ stick celery, chopped
50 g (2 oz) smoked tofu,
  finely chopped
4 tablespoons tomato purée

225 g (8 oz) continental lentils
2 stock cubes
150 ml (¼ pint) medium red wine
1 tablespoon thyme leaves
salt
freshly ground black pepper

Heat the oil in a large saucepan and fry the onion, carrot and celery until slightly browned. Add the tofu and cook for another minute.

Stir in the remaining ingredients with 750 ml (1¼ pints) water. Bring to a full boil. Reduce the heat, then cover with a lid and simmer for 20 minutes or until the lentils are cooked but not mushy.

Continue cooking uncovered until all the liquid is absorbed. Adjust the seasoning.

Serve with *Pommes Amandine* page 121 and any leafy green vegetable.

CASSOULET AU PAYS BASQUE

SERVES 4

A stew-like soup which is an adaptation of the famous Cassoulet originating from Castelnaudary on the Canal du Midi and is a meal in one.

225 g (8 oz) haricots beans
450 g (1 lb) baking potatoes, peeled and cut into large chunks.
1 clove garlic, crushed with a little salt
6 shallots, peeled and divided
2 medium leeks, trimmed and sliced.
10–12 black olives, stoned and sliced
2 tablespoons chopped fresh parsley
1 large lovage leaf, finely scissored
(celery leaf can be used as a substitute)
600 ml (1 pint) well-flavoured stock
2 teaspoons olive oil
freshly ground black pepper
salt
1 small white loaf
50 g (2 oz) butter or margarine
paprika

Soak the beans in cold water overnight. Bring to the boil in a large pan of fresh water and boil rapidly for 10 minutes. Drain. Return to the saucepan, adding the potatoes, garlic, shallots, leeks, olives, chopped parsley and lovage. Pour in the stock and add the oil.

Bring to the boil, reduce the heat, cover and simmer for 2 hours. Top up with more stock if needed and season with freshly ground black pepper and salt. Cook until the beans are soft, then boil rapidly to reduce liquid until the cassoulet has thickened.

Pre-heat the oven to gas mark 4, 350°F (180°C).

During the last half hour cut a lengthways crust from the loaf and pull out cotton wool ball-sized pieces from the inside. Space the balls out in a baking dish, melt the butter, then pour over and bake for 15–20 minutes until golden brown.

Garnish individual soup portions with 2–3 crusty bread balls and sprinkle with a little paprika.

CHILLI WITH GUACAMOLE

SERVES 4

In the USA chilli is more like a thick soup and is served in a bowl. The dish takes it name from the spice which can vary in strength from the milder compound chilli powder, containing other spices, to the hottest pure cayenne. Read the label on the carton carefully to see which you are buying. When cooked this recipe has little surplus liquid, making it more suitable to be served on a dinner plate. The cool guacamole contrasts with the heat of the chilli.

1–2 tablespoons vegetable oil
1 large onion, finely chopped
1 clove garlic, finely chopped with a
  little salt
1 teaspoon fennel seeds
1½ teaspoons compound chilli powder
1 teaspoon ground cumin
397 g (14 oz) can chopped tomatoes
225 g (8 oz) canned or bottled
  pimentos, drained and sliced
150 ml (¼ pint) medium red wine
4 small bay leaves

400 g (14 oz) cooked kidney beans
salt
freshly ground black pepper

Guacamole ....
2 avocados
1 shallot
1 clove garlic
2 tablespoons fresh lemon juice
salt
freshly ground black pepper

Heat the oil in a large frying-pan and fry the onion and garlic until brown. Add the fennel seeds, compound chilli powder and cumin and cook for 30 seconds. Stir in the tomatoes, pimentos, wine and bay leaves. Bring to the boil and without covering, simmer until thick.

Mix in the kidney beans and continue cooking until they are thoroughly heated. Season to taste with salt and pepper and add 4–5 tablespoons water. Crush mixture lightly with a potato masher.

While the chilli is cooking make the guacamole. Halve, stone and peel the avocados, cut up and purée in a food processor with the shallot, garlic, lemon juice and seasoning.

Place chilli on warm plates and pour the guacamole sauce over the top.

Serve immediately with *Flour Tortillas* page 152, briefly warmed in the oven and a crisp green salad.

DHAL

SERVES 4

Dhal *is somewhat like split pea purée – highly nutritious. It thickens as it cools so that if it is to be frozen extra liquid will be needed when reheating to prevent the* Dhal *drying and sticking to the pan.*

175 g (6 oz) yellow split peas, rinsed and soaked if packet directs
1 teaspoon turmeric
½ teaspoon ground ginger
1 tablespoon garam masala
2 bay leaves

1 onion, chopped
1 clove garlic, crushed
2–3 tablespoons sunflower oil
salt
freshly ground black pepper

Put the split peas in a heavy based saucepan with 600 ml (1 pint) water. Bring to the boil, then simmer uncovered for 30 minutes, skimming when necessary.

Stir in the turmeric, ginger, garam masala and bay leaves and continue cooking for 30 minutes or until the split peas are soft.

Meanwhile fry the onion and garlic in the oil until crisp and brown but not burnt. Drain on kitchen paper.

Remove the bay leaves and mash or purée the split peas with any remaining liquid and season with salt and pepper. If you like a very thin Dhal add a little extra stock but if a thicker texture is preferred, return to the pan and cook over low heat until most of the moisture has been absorbed.

Stir in half the onions, pour into a serving bowl and garnish with the remaining onions.

Serve as part of a 'Curry Dinner' with *Cauliflower and Potato Bhajis* page 19 and *Samosas* page 70

GREEN LENTIL COURGETTES

SERVES 4

At their best, courgettes have an even coloured dark green skin which can easily be pierced with a fingernail. Avoid them if they have soft patches or are shrivelled at the stalk end. Damaged or stale courgettes can be extremely bitter and will spoil the flavour of the topping.

8 × 15 cm (6 in) courgettes,
  rinsed and dried
175 g (6 oz) cooked green lentils
4 spring onions, finely sliced
1 medium-size green pepper,
  de-seeded and finely chopped
1 tomato, chopped
1 teaspoon fresh lemon thyme leaves,
  finely scissored

4–5 tablespoons grated roasted
  hazelnuts
1 teaspoon olive oil
salt
freshly ground black pepper
½ teaspoon sweet paprika

Pre-heat the oven to gas mark 5, 375°F (190°C).

Halve each courgette lengthwise. Scoop out the flesh with a teaspoon or grapefruit knife leaving 5 mm (1¼ in) walls. Finely chop the flesh and mix in a bowl with the lentils, spring onions, green pepper, tomato, thyme, hazelnuts and olive oil, seasoning to taste with salt and pepper.

Pile the mixture into the courgette shells and place on a lightly buttered baking tray. Bake for 25 minutes, then raise the temperature to Gas mark 7, 425°F (220°C) for 4–6 minutes until brown on top.

Sprinkle with paprika. Serve with *Duchesse Potatoes* page 110 and *Savoy Cabbage and Tomato Fricassée* page 126.

INDIVIDUAL BEAN AND ONION GRATINÉS

SERVES 4

As this recipe is finished under the grill, the individual pots you choose must be flame-proof and ideally be only slightly larger in diameter than the French bread topping.

50 g (2 oz) butter or margarine	300 ml (½ pint) red wine
1 clove garlic, finely sliced	100 g (4 oz) borlotti beans
4–6 large onions, finely sliced	freshly ground black pepper
1 litre (1¾ pints), well-flavoured stock, preferably home-made	2.5 cm (1 in) thick slices French bread
2 tablespoons grated Parmesan cheese	100 g (4 oz) grated Gruyère cheese

Melt the butter or margarine in a large saucepan and sauté the garlic and onions over moderate heat, adding a few slices at a time to prevent lowering the temperature until they become a rich golden colour. This is important to develop a good colour and flavour and takes 15–20 minutes.

Meanwhile bring the stock to the boil and pour on to the onions. Simmer for 30 minutes.

Add the Parmesan, wine and beans and continue cooking until the onions are in a thick liquid which forms a skin on top. Season with the pepper to taste.

Heat four or five individual flame-proof bowls. Light the grill and toast the bread on one side.

Fill the bowls with the soup. Float the bread toasted side down on the soup, top with the Gruyère and brown rapidly under the grill.

Serve with extra toast or *Garlic Bread Nuggets* page 153, *Lemon Dressed Green Salad* page 146 and *Minted Tomato Salad* page 147.

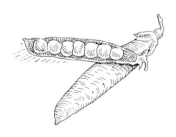

MUNG BEAN "MEAT" BALLS
IN ESPAGNOLE SAUCE

SERVES 4

Canned mushroom soup darkened with a few drops of gravy browning can be used instead of Espagnole Sauce *page 131 if pressed for time. For similar reasons I have included Dutch-style tea rusks because they can be crushed so easily in the hands. Mung beans when cooked have a similar texture to that of cooked lentils.*

225 g (8 oz) mung beans
1 tablespoon sunflower oil
1 small onion, finely chopped
⅛ teaspoon garlic paste or 1 small
  clove garlic, crushed
2 teaspoons turmeric
1 teaspoon paprika
4 small mushrooms, finely chopped

1 tomato, finely chopped
salt
freshly ground black pepper
2–3 tea rusks
1 egg, beaten
450 ml (¾ pint) *Espagnole Sauce* page
  131 or canned mushroom soup

Rinse the mung beans, bring to the boil in a pan of unsalted water and cook rapidly for 10 minutes. Skim if necessary and drain.

Pre-heat the oven to gas mark 6, 400°F (200°C).

Heat the oil and fry the onion until soft, add the garlic, turmeric and paprika and cook, stirring briskly for 30 seconds. Mix in the mushrooms and tomato, 750 ml (1¼ pints) water and the drained mung beans. Bring to the boil, then reduce the heat and simmer for 20 minutes or until the beans are tender and only a tablespoon of liquid remains.

Crush and mix in two of the rusks, season with salt and pepper and bind with the egg, adding the third rusk only if needed to form a soft shapeable mixture.

Pour the *Espagnole Sauce* or mushroom soup into a large shallow ovenproof dish and stir in 1–2 tablespoons water. Form the mung meat mixture into 10–12 balls and arrange them in the dish in a single layer. Bake for 30 minutes, basting occasionally with the sauce.

Serve with *Braised Celery* page 106 and *Fantailed Potatoes* page 111.

ONION AND LENTIL BURGERS

SERVES 4

Split red lentils are the fastest cooking of any of the pulse family. They do not need soaking, although it is a good idea to rinse them in several changes of cold water to reduce foaming and the formation of scum. Cook them in a saucepan for about 25 minutes or use a pressure cooker or microwave. I cook one pound at a time and freeze in the quantities likely to be required.

50 g (2 oz) red lentils
1 large onion, finely chopped
½ stock cube
1 tablespoon tomato purée
½ teaspoon turmeric

salt
freshly ground black pepper
½ beaten egg
175 g (6 oz) porridge oats
sunflower oil

Cook the lentils according to the directions on the packet, adding the onion and stock cube when half of the water has been absorbed.

When the lentils are tender, drain thoroughly but do not mash.

Return the mixture to the pan and stir in the tomato purée and turmeric. Season to taste.

Leave to cool for ten minutes before mixing in the egg, then refrigerate for 15 minutes to firm up the mixture.

Spread the porridge oats on a sheet of non-stick parchment. Shape the lentil mix into eight burgers and coat with the porridge oats, pressing them in with a palette knife.

Heat about 2 cm (¾ in) fresh cooking oil in a large frying pan and fry the burgers until thoroughly heated and golden brown. Reduce the heat if the burgers seem to be browning too quickly.

Serve hot with *Quick Tomato Sauce* page 133, boiled new potatoes and Brussels sprouts.

SHEPHERD'S KIDNEY BEAN PIE

SERVES 4

You get about 250 g (9 oz) kidney beans from a 400 g (14 oz) can which is a point to be remembered if home-cooked beans are preferred.

400 g (14 oz) can red kidney beans	½ teaspoon salt
2 tablespoons sunflower oil	¼ teaspoon freshly ground black
2 medium onions, finely sliced	pepper
1 clove garlic, crushed	225 g (8 oz) can chopped tomatoes
⅛ teaspoon chilli powder	1 teaspoon gravy granules
¾ teaspoon ground cumin	450 g (1 lb) mashed potato

Pre-heat the oven to gas mark 6, 400°F (200°C).

Rinse the kidney beans and drain thoroughly.

Heat the oil in a saucepan (preferably non-stick) and fry the onions until soft and just coloured. Add the garlic, chilli powder, cumin, salt and pepper and cook for 1 minute. Stir in the kidney beans and cook, stirring continuously for 3–4 minutes until all the oil is absorbed.

Crush lightly with a potato masher. Transfer the mixture to a flame-proof dish.

Mix the tomatoes and gravy granules in the pan and bring to the boil. Pour over the kidney beans and top with the potato. Ridge with a fork.

Bake until the potatoes are brown, about 30 minutes. Serve with *Espagnole Sauce* page 131, spring greens and diced swede.

Quorn, Tofu and Nuts

BROWN CAP MUSHROOM AND BEAN CURD
STROGANOFF

SERVES 4

Brown cap mushrooms are firmer than the white. They are regularly on the vegetable displays but white mushrooms can be substituted if necessary. The silken type of tofu is better for this recipe but does tend to break up after slicing, so treat the uncooked strips gently.

1 × 250 g (9 oz) pack firm tofu
25 g (1 oz) butter
3 tablespoons vegetable oil
225 g (8 oz) onions, thinly sliced
275 g (10 oz) brown cap mushrooms,
  quartered
5 tablespoons Madeira or sweet sherry

150 ml (5 fl oz) soured cream or
  Greek-style yogurt
grated rind of 1 lemon
2 teaspoons fresh chervil, chopped
salt
freshly ground black pepper

Press the tofu between kitchen paper to remove surplus liquid. Slice, then cut into thin strips and spread them out on a large plate.

Heat the butter and 2 tablespoons of the oil in a large frying-pan and fry the onion until golden. Carefully add the tofu, a few strips at a time, ensuring that they do not stick together. Turn them over frequently with a fish slice until they are brown. As tofu fries it splatters so be careful.

Remove the tofu and onion from the pan, add the remaining oil and the mushrooms and cook for 2–3 minutes. Stir in the wine, replace the tofu and onion in the pan and reheat for a minute or two.

Fold in the soured cream or yogurt, lemon rind and chopped chervil. Adjust the seasoning and spoon into the centre of a heated shallow serving dish.

Serve with a border of freshly cooked rice, *Medley of Green Beans* page 117 and steamed broccoli.

CHESTNUT STUFFED CABBAGE

SERVES 4

Chestnuts and cabbage go well together. I have used canned natural chestnut purée but when chestnuts are in season and you have the time to spare, split and stew them after peeling and mash, adding extra stock.

1 green cabbage weighing about 1 kg (2 lb)
200 g (7 oz) canned natural chestnut purée
50 g (2 oz) fresh wholemeal breadcrumbs
25 g (1 oz) polyunsaturated margarine
1 dessert apple, peeled, cored and chopped

¼ teaspoon ground allspice
4 tablespoons red wine
1 teaspoon olive oil
2 tablespoons apple juice
pinch of sugar
salt
freshly ground black pepper

Pre-heat the oven to gas mark 5, 375°F (190°C).

Cut off the base of the cabbage so that it will balance steadily, then remove and discard the outer leaves. To make a deep well, remove the centre leaves with a small sharp knife. Shred these finely and blanch in boiling water for 2 minutes. Drain and reserve.

Mix the purée, breadcrumbs, margarine, apple, allspice and wine together, season well with salt and pepper and crush with a potato masher. Pack into the cabbage hollow. Dot the top with extra margarine.

Stand the cabbage on a large piece of foil, pull up the edges and twist the top to secure dolly-bag fashion. Place on a rack in a baking tin and bake for 45 minutes.

Open the foil at the top to expose the stuffing and continue baking for 15 minutes to brown the top.

Put the oil in a small saucepan and stir in the blanched shredded cabbage. Cook, stirring until hot, then add the apple juice and season with sugar, salt and pepper.

Serve the stuffed cabbage, with some of the shredded cabbage on the side of the plates, *Tabbouleh* (omitting the olives) page 149 and *Roast Pumpkin* page 125.

CHOP SUEY WITH WATER CHESTNUTS

SERVES 4

Chop Suey in the Mandarin language means 'mixed fragments' and is not an authentic dish in its own right. We in the West have enjoyed eating it for many years now and its great advantage is that it is so quick and easy to prepare.

3 tablespoons dark soy sauce
2 tablespoons dry sherry
250 g (9 oz) Quorn
2 tablespoons vegetable oil
1 medium onion, sliced
1 clove garlic, crushed
2.5 cm (1 in) piece ginger root,
  finely chopped
½ teaspoon Chinese five spice powder

2 sticks celery, sliced
1 small red pepper, de-seeded
  and diced
1 small green pepper, de-seeded and
  cut into thin strips
50 g (2 oz) water chestnuts, sliced
1 large flat mushroom, chopped
250 g (9 oz) fresh beansprouts
1 tablespoon cornflour

Mix the soy sauce and the sherry, stir in the Quorn and leave for 30 minutes.

Heat the oil in a large frying-pan and stir-fry the onion, garlic, ginger and five spice for 2 minutes. Add the celery and peppers and stir-fry for 2–3 minutes, then mix in the water chestnuts, mushroom, beansprouts and Quorn together with the marinade.

Cook for a few more minutes, then add the cornflour blended with 3 tablespoons cold water and cook, stirring until the mixture thickens.

Serve with freshly boiled Chinese noodles and prawn crackers.

DEVILLED QUORN

SERVES 4

Quorn with its meaty texture and breast of chicken colour takes on the flavour of the marinade or sauce it is cooked with. Ideal for the vegetarian, it is also particularly low in calories and so can be slipped into meat dishes to balance the cholesterol and calorie content.

2 teaspoons made English mustard

1 tablespoon Worcestershire sauce or
  vegetarian equivalent

2 teaspoons vegetable oil

1 teaspoon paprika

1 teaspoon coarsely ground black
  pepper

1 teaspoon salt

250 g (9 oz) Quorn

15 g (½ oz) butter

Blend the mustard, Worcestershire sauce, oil, paprika, pepper and salt together in a bowl. Add the Quorn and toss until well coated. Cover and leave for 1 hour, stirring occasionally.

Remove the rack from the grill pan and put in the butter. Melt under moderate heat. Add the Quorn cubes, toss to coat with the butter and cook on all sides for a few minutes until piping hot.

Serve with buttered tagliatelle, mangetout and grilled tomatoes.

GRILLED SMOKED TOFU STEAKS

SERVES 4

Smoked tofu has a grand flavour of its own, but is even tastier if brushed with this tomatoey marinade during cooking.

6 tablespoons olive oil

2 tablespoons tomato purée

½ teaspoon ground ginger

½ teaspoon turmeric

¼ teaspoon freshly ground black
  pepper

2 × 250 g (9 oz) packets smoked tofu

Remove the rack and pour two tablespoons of the oil into the grill pan, making sure that it spreads evenly over the base.

Mix the remaining oil, tomato purée and spices together.

Cut the tofu in half, then slice horizontally to produce 4 thick steaks. Place in a single layer in the grill pan and brush with the marinade.

Prepare a moderate grill and cook the steaks for 5 minutes. Using a fish slice carefully turn the steaks over and baste the tops as before.

Grill for 10 minutes, basting frequently and serve hot with *Ratatouille* page 122 and green tagliatelle.

NORFOLK KEBABS

SERVES 4

The portions for these kebabs are large, so you will need really long skewers to hold all the ingredients.

1 large courgette, topped and tailed
1 orange pepper, de-seeded
8 baby onions
12 baby tomatoes, pierced once
225 g (8 oz) Quorn chunks

3 tablespoons vegetable oil
2 tablespoons horseradish sauce
2 tablespoons tomato purée
¼ teaspoon sweet paprika

Halve the courgette lengthwise and cut into 1 cm (½ in) slices. Cut the orange pepper into bite-sized pieces.

Thread the onions, pepper, courgette, tomatoes and Quorn on to four skewers so that the colours alternate and the onions are at either end.

Pre-heat a moderate grill and line a grill pan with foil.

Combine the oil, horseradish sauce, tomato purée and paprika and brush over the kebabs. Place on the foil and grill until tender for about 15 minutes, turning the skewers and basting from time to time.

Serve with *Saffron Rice* page 126 and *Braised Leeks in Lemon and Soured Cream Sauce* page 107.

NUT CUTLETS – YES!

SERVES 4

Yes! I am proud to include this recipe for a much derided vegetarian dish. Try it, giving the recipe another name if you think your family won't eat it with my title! Non-vegetarians will enjoy them even more if you add that well known beef stock beverage, or use a dark coloured vegetable stock cube.

25 g (1 oz) butter or margarine
1 tablespoon sunflower oil
1 onion, very finely chopped
2 celery sticks, very finely chopped
1 carrot, grated or very finely chopped
100 g (4 oz) roasted hazelnuts,
  skinned and finely ground
150 ml (¼ pint) strong stock

75 g (3 oz) bulgar (cracked wheat)
1 tablespoon sweet pickle
1 tablespoon grated Parmesan cheese
salt
freshly ground black pepper
2 eggs, beaten
flour
vegetable oil

Heat the butter and oil in a large saucepan and fry the onion, celery and carrot until soft and just beginning to brown. Add the nuts and cook for another minute.

Stir in the stock, bring to the boil and mix in the bulgar. Cover and remove from the heat.

Add the pickle and Parmesan, and season lightly with salt and pepper.

When cool mix in the egg. Shape into four or eight cutlets on a floured surface. Fry or grill in an oiled pan for 2–3 minutes on each side until brown, using a fish slice to avoid breaking them up.

Serve with *Spicy Spinach* page 127 and *Baked Piperade* page 105.

QUORN AND PEA DHANSAK

SERVES 4

Quorn is a new food without animal fats or cholesterol. It is harvested from a tiny plant and contains myco-protein, egg white and vegetable flavourings. Since it has a freezer life of three months and needs practically no preparation it comes in handy for the busy cook. Non-vegetarians will not detect the omission of meat in this dish.

2 tablespoons vegetable oil	150 ml (5 fl oz) natural yogurt
1 teaspoon cumin seeds	450 ml (¾ pint) stock
2 cloves garlic, crushed	2 tablespoons desiccated coconut
1 large onion, finely chopped	4 heaped tablespoons frozen peas
½ teaspoon ground ginger	250 g (9 oz) carton Quorn
¼ teaspoon turmeric	1 tablespoon cornflour
2 tablespoons bottled mild curry paste	4 tablespoons double cream

Heat the oil in a saucepan and fry the cumin seeds for 20–30 seconds. Add the garlic and onion and cook until golden brown, then stir in the ginger, turmeric, curry paste and yogurt.

Add the stock and coconut, bring to the boil, then reduce the heat and simmer uncovered for 15 minutes, stirring occasionally.

Add the peas and cook for 3–4 minutes. Add the Quorn.

Blend the cornflour with the cream and 2 tablespoons cold water. Stir into the pan and bring back to the boil, stirring continuously. Reduce the heat and simmer for 3 minutes.

Serve with *Saffron Rice* page 126 and sliced tomatoes sprinkled with salt, freshly ground black pepper and coriander.

TANDOORI TIKKA

SERVES 4

A Tikka dish consists of marinated ingredients which are subsequently grilled, the effect being similar to barbecuing.

vegetable oil
1 large onion, chopped
250 g (9 oz) pack firm Tofu, pressed
  dry on kitchen paper, then cubed
3 tablespoons flaked almonds
3 tablespoons natural yogurt
4 tablespoons bottled tandoori

flavoured paste
1 teaspoon fresh coriander, scissored
175 g (6 oz) cauliflower florets
8 okra, topped and tailed
1 courgette, cut into chunks
2 tablespoons single cream

Heat about 3 tablespoons of oil in a frying-pan and cook the onion until golden in colour.

Add the tofu, two or three cubes at a time, and fry on all sides. Gently stir in the almonds and cook for another minute.

Remove from the heat and stir in the yogurt, tandoori paste and coriander, taking care not to break up the tofu.

Crisp-cook the cauliflower, okra and courgette in boiling salted water, drain thoroughly and add to the frying-pan. Stir to coat with the paste, cover and leave for 2 hours.

Remove the rack and spoon the ingredients into a grill pan. Spread out and cook under moderate heat until the marinade has dried out.

Add the cream, tossing to coat the tofu and vegetables. Serve at once with *Pilau Rice* page 120, *Cucumber Raita* page 140 and *Curried Egg Salad* page 140.

WALNUT AND PARMESAN BREAD AND BUTTER PUDDING

SERVES 4

Savoury bread and butter pudding is a scrumptious crispy topped, low-cost pudding. Sliced square Hovis has just the right texture and thickness but thin slices from any similar size brown loaf will do. Add a few shakes of cayenne pepper if you prefer a hot and spicy dish.

50 g (2 oz) shelled walnuts, coarsely chopped.
6 slices Hovis from a cut loaf
butter or margarine
6 tablespoons grated Parmesan cheese
2 tablespoons fresh marjoram leaves, finely scissored

1 large egg plus 1 yolk
300 ml (½ pint) milk
salt
freshly ground black pepper

Pre-heat the oven to gas mark 4, 350°F (180°C).

Put the walnuts in a small pan, cover with cold water, then bring to the boil. Place in a strainer, rinse under cold running water and drain thoroughly.

Toast the bread, leave to cool, then butter on one side. Cut the slices into four triangles.

Butter a 23 cm (9 in) oval pie dish and cover the base with some of the triangles, buttered side uppermost. Sprinkle with 2 tablespoons of Parmesan, some marjoram and a quarter of the walnuts. Repeat the layering, finishing with the remaining walnuts.

Beat the egg and extra yolk into the milk and season with salt and pepper. Strain evenly over the top of the dish and leave to soak in for about 30 minutes.

Place the dish in a roasting tin and pour hot water into the tin to reach half-way up the dish. Bake for 35–40 minutes until no juices run free when a table knife is inserted through the centre and the top is brown and crisp. Serve with *Petits Pois à la Française* page 118 and *Creamed Spinach* page 109.

COMPANION VEGETABLES AND SAUCES

The vegetables in this chapter are more interesting than everyday ones cooked by steaming or boiling. No one can deny the joy of eating properly cooked British-style vegetables, but it does make a change to have something a little different. The recipes given here are just that, and should be used to enhance and complement the main dishes. I have made some suggestions at the end of each main dish recipe to help you decide what to serve. When making your own choice, try and pick those with contrasting colour and texture and check that the main ingredients are not similar to those in the companion dishes.

When cooking the vegetables, instead of throwing away the cooking liquid, strain rather than drain the vegetables and save the liquid for stocks. Another useful way to stock pile is to simmer the outside leaves of greens and cauliflower and tops of spring onion stalks, until the liquid is considerably reduced, to concentrate the flavour and add seasonings to taste.

In the wider context of the book, I have classified rice, pasta and grains as vegetables, to offer more variety and nutritional, balanced meals. With the variety of gravies and sauces in the latter part of this chapter, there should be all you need to bring out the best in the Main Courses, and enable you to create *Veg and 2 Veg* dishes for any occasion.

Companion Vegetables

BAKED PIPERADE

SERVES 4

A flameproof casserole can be put safely under the grill, confining the eventual washing up to a minimum. Increase the ingredients and add extras such as cooked red kidney or black-eye beans, mixing them in well to prevent drying out and serve as a main course.

1 green pepper
1 red pepper
2 tomatoes, quartered
1 large onion, finely chopped
1 teaspoon mild paprika

2 tablespoons olive oil
salt
freshly ground black pepper
4 eggs

Pre-heat the oven to gas mark 7, 425°F (220°C).

Grill the peppers until the skins blister. Wrap them in greaseproof paper for 10 minutes before de-seeding and peeling. Slice into thin strips.

Combine the tomatoes, onion, paprika and peppers in the oil in a flameproof casserole dish, baking for about 10 minutes until tender. Season with salt and pepper.

Make four hollows in the mixture and break an egg into each. Cover with the lid if wished and continue baking for about 5 minutes until the eggs are cooked to taste.

BAKED TOMATOES

SERVES 4

The tomato is a universal favourite, with no cholesterol and a high energy value. The beef tomato is comparatively new but it lives up to its name, being fleshy and substantial. Be careful if re-heating as tomatoes collapse suddenly.

2 beef tomatoes, halved crossways	pinch of caster sugar
2 teaspoons medium red wine	butter or margarine
freshly ground black pepper	1 tablespoon chopped fresh parsley

Pre-heat the oven to gas mark 4, 350°F (180°C).

Arrange the tomatoes cut side uppermost in a single layer in a lightly buttered baking dish in which the tomatoes will fit snugly. Sprinkle over the wine and season with the pepper and a pinch of sugar. Dot with butter or margarine.

Bake in the centre of the oven for 15–20 minutes until tender. Sprinkle with the parsley and serve hot.

BRAISED CELERY

SERVES 4

Celery is available throughout the year. Sometimes the leaves have been removed, which is a shame as they are really useful for flavouring casseroles and soups. The paler leaves are mildly flavoured and I recommend that they are included in the recipe.

1 large head of celery	300 (½ pint) boiling water
4–5 spring onions, finely sliced	2 teaspoons olive oil
1 bay leaf	salt
1 stock cube	freshly ground black pepper

Pre-heat the oven to gas mark 4, 350°F (180°C).

Cut away the thick base of the celery. Chop the smaller leaves, trim the tops from the celery sticks and cut into finger-sized lengths. Scrape or peel away the strings from the coarser stalks.

Combine all the ingredients in a saucepan, bring to the boil and cook for 3 minutes.

Transfer to a shallow casserole dish, arranging the celery in layers. Cover with buttered greaseproof paper and bake for 30–35 minutes until the celery is tender and only a few spoons of thin sauce remain.

BRAISED LEEKS IN LEMON AND SOURED CREAM SAUCE

SERVES 4

Large leeks can be tough and squeaky. In the event that no young ones are obtainable, halve lengthwise and blanch for 2–4 minutes before baking.

250 ml (8 fl oz) stock
grated rind and juice of 1 small lemon
8 slender leeks, trimmed
salt
freshly ground black pepper

25 g (1 oz) butter or margarine
25 g (1 oz) plain flour
150 ml (¼ pint) soured cream
1 tablespoon chopped shelled
 pistachio nuts

Pre-heat the oven to gas mark 4, 350°F (180°C).

Mix the stock, lemon rind and juice in a large shallow casserole dish and add the leeks, placing them in a single layer. Season with salt and pepper. Cover tightly and bake for 30–40 minutes until tender.

Strain, reserving 250 ml (8 fl oz) of the liquid. Should there be insufficient add a little water or white wine.

Melt the butter in a small saucepan over moderate heat, stir in the flour and cook, stirring for 1 minute. Pour in the reserved liquid and cook, stirring until thickened.

Add the soured cream and remove from the heat when reheated but not boiling, which might cause the sauce to curdle. Adjust the seasoning.

Pour the sauce over the leeks and sprinkle with chopped pistachio nuts.

CARAMEL GLAZED BABY ONIONS

SERVES 4

Pickling onions can take the place of button or baby onions but the tiny silver onions are really too small.

450 g (1 lb) baby onions
1 tablespoon sunflower oil
3 tablespoons clear honey

150 ml (¼ pint) well-flavoured stock
1 tablespoon red wine vinegar
1 tablespoon medium sherry

Peel the onions and put into a heavy-based saucepan with the oil. Cook over moderate heat, tossing the onions vigorously until glossy and just beginning to colour.

Add 2 tablespoons of the honey and cook, stirring constantly until the onions are golden brown.

Pour in the stock, vinegar and sherry. Bring rapidly to the boil, then reduce the heat and simmer uncovered, tossing frequently until most of the liquid has evaporated and the onions begin to brown and crisp. Stir in remaining honey.

CARIBBEAN RICE

SERVES 4–6

This fruity rice dish goes well with roasts, grills, fried pasties, burgers or curries. Do not let a lack of pineapple and lychees deter you from cooking this recipe as the rice, when cooked in this way, is undeniably delicious.

225 g (8 oz) easy cook long grain rice
50 g (2 oz) desiccated coconut
salt
150 ml (¼ pint) orange juice

6 fresh lychees, peeled, stoned and
  coarsely chopped
1 thick slice fresh pineapple, coarsely
  chopped

Cook the rice and coconut in plenty of boiling salted water for 10 minutes or until a part-cooked grain can be broken cleanly with a knife. Drain thoroughly and return to the pan.

Pour in the orange juice and simmer covered until the juice is mostly absorbed, about 5 minutes.

Mix in the lychees and pineapple and warm through over low heat.

CREAMED SPINACH

SERVES 4

A point to remember is that cooked spinach weighs only about a third of its original weight. Bear this is mind if you decide to use frozen chopped spinach which contains a lot of water already. Canned spinach is not suitable as it alters the flavour.

900 g (2 lb) spinach

Sauce ....
15 g (½ oz) butter or margarine
2 tablespoons flour
150 ml (¼ pint) milk

salt
freshly ground black pepper
pinch nutmeg
2 tablespoons double cream (optional)

Wash the spinach in several changes of cold water. Remove the coarse stems. Adding only 1 tablespoon of water cook the spinach in a covered saucepan over low heat, shaking the pan from time to time to prevent sticking.

Drain and chop the spinach finely by hand or in the food processor. Drain once more.

Melt the butter or margarine in a large saucepan over low heat. Stir in the flour and cook for 1 minute, stirring continuously. Gradually beat in the milk and cook, still stirring, until the sauce thickens. Season with salt and pepper and add the nutmeg.

Beat in the spinach until smooth and cook for 2–3 minutes. Adjust the seasoning and stir in the cream if using.

CRISPY ONION RINGS

SERVES 2–3

Even frozen battered onion rings have to be cooked and are certainly not as nice as when you start with fresh onions. These are crispier since they have not been denatured by the freezing process. However, I find very little difference between using home-made or made up dry-mix batter in the finished product.

Batter ....
150 g (5 oz) plain flour
1 large egg
200 ml (7 fl oz) milk
....
6 tablespoons fresh breadcrumbs

3 tablespoons sesame seeds
salt
freshly ground black pepper
3 large onions
oil for deep frying

Sift the flour into a bowl. Make a well in the centre and add the egg and milk beating them into the flour to form a smooth batter.

Mix the breadcrumbs and sesame seeds into the batter and season with salt and pepper.

Thickly slice the onions and separate into rings (use up the smaller centre ones in another recipe).

Dip the onion rings in the batter and deep fry a few at a time, turning them over when they rise to the surface. Remove them as soon as they are ready and drain on kitchen paper.

DUCHESSE POTATOES

SERVES 4

Vary the recipe by adding chopped nuts to the mixture and topping with blanched almonds or mixing in fresh chopped chives. If you wish, tuck a cherry tomato into the centre of the mixture when piping to give a hidden surprise.

1 kg (2 lb) potatoes, peeled
40 g (1½ oz) butter or margarine
2 eggs, beaten

4–5 tablespoons milk
salt
freshly ground black pepper

Pre-heat the oven to gas mark 6, 400°F (200°C).

Put a 1 cm (½ in) star piping tube into a large piping bag. Butter or line a baking tray with non-stick parchment.

Cut up the potatoes and cook in boiling salted water until tender.

Drain and mash thoroughly with the butter. A food processor is not suitable. Leave for a few moments, then mix in half of the egg.

Return the potato to the saucepan and stir over the lowest heat for 1–2 minutes, adding the milk gradually. Season with salt and pepper to taste.

Spoon into the prepared piping bag and press to close up any gaps in the mixture. Pipe small pyramids of potato about 2.5 cm (1 in) in diameter on to the baking tray, topping with a potato star. Leave to cool.

Brush with the remaining beaten egg and bake for 5–10 minutes until pale golden.

FANTAILED POTATOES

SERVES 4

Make sure that the oven temperature is not too high or the milk will form a dark skin. This is in no way unpalatable but some people object to it.

8 medium size 100 g (4 oz) potatoes	salt
40 g (1½ oz) butter or margarine	freshly ground black pepper
300 ml (½ pint) milk	

Pre-heat the oven to gas mark 4, 350°F (180°C).

Peel the potatoes and cut a slice from each so that they will stand upright. Make 5 or 6 vertical slits in each potato from the top not quite to the bottom so that the slices are not completely severed.

Put the butter or margarine in a roasting tin, heat in the oven until melted, then put the potatoes in the tin and thoroughly baste them with the melted fat.

Warm the milk and 150 ml (¼ pt) of water and season with salt and pepper. Pour into the dish.

Bake for 1–1¼ hours, basting occasionally with the milk and gently squeezing the bases with tongs to help open out the slices.

GARLIC AND FINES HERBES BAKED MUSHROOMS

SERVES 4–6

Although this is included as a side vegetable, the recipe can be increased to take the place of a main dish.

12 medium size open cup mushrooms
4 tablespoons olive oil
150 ml (¼ pint) stock
2 tablespoons fresh lemon juice
salt
freshly ground black pepper
15 g (½ oz) butter
2 tablespoons mixed chopped fresh

herbs including parsley, chives,
sage and basil
2–3 cloves garlic, crushed
pinch of nutmeg
75 g (3 oz) dried breadcrumbs

Slice away the mushroom stalks, chop them finely and mix with the oil, stock and half of the lemon juice. Season with salt and pepper and leave to marinate for 1 hour.

Pre-heat the oven to gas mark 5, 375°F (190°C).

Heat the butter in a frying-pan and sauté the mushroom caps on each side for 2–3 minutes. Remove from the pan and set aside.

Put the stalk mixture in the pan and cook over moderate heat until soft. Stir in the herbs, garlic, nutmeg and dried breadcrumbs and adjust the seasoning.

Pile the mixture on to the flat side of the mushrooms and shape into domes. Sprinkle with the remaining lemon juice.

Arrange the mushrooms in a single layer in a shallow baking dish and bake for 20–25 minutes until the topping begins to brown.

GARLIC SAUTÉ MUSHROOMS

SERVES 4

This is one of the easiest and most impressive side vegetables to prepare. It allows plenty of room for experimentation. Vary the herbs and mix in flaked almonds, cashew nuts, peanuts or chick peas or add diced or small vegetables such as petits pois, green beans or tiny brown bread croûtons. The dish may be cooked up to an hour in advance and can be kept in the covered pan away from the heat to be quickly re-heated when required.

450 g (1 lb) small mushrooms
4 spring onions, white part only
1–2 cloves garlic, peeled
1–2 tablespoons virgin olive oil

1 tablespoon chopped fresh basil
  leaves
salt
freshly ground black pepper

Wipe and quarter the mushrooms, finely slice both the spring onions and the garlic.

Heat the oil in a large frying-pan, add the mushrooms, spring onions and garlic and fry for a few minutes, tossing the vegetables so that all are well coated with oil.

Reduce the heat and stir in the basil, seasoning sparingly with salt and generously with black pepper.

Cover with a lid and cook gently for 10 minutes.

GRILLED SEASONAL VEGETABLES

SERVES 4

A selection of colourful vegetables ready-cooked for eating with a fork, make an ideal accompaniment to rice and pasta dishes.

1 red pepper	16 baby onions, peeled
1 yellow pepper	3 tablespoons olive oil
1 green pepper	1 teaspoon hazelnut oil
225 g (8 oz) butternut or acorn squash	1 tablespoon chopped rosemary leaves
4 slender leeks, white part only	salt
2 firm courgettes	freshly ground black pepper

Core and de-seed the peppers and cut into bite-sized pieces. Peel and de-seed the squash and cut into small chunks. Thickly slice the leeks, and top, tail and thickly slice the courgettes.

Bring a pan of salted water to the boil and cook the leeks, onions and squash for 3 minutes, add the courgettes and cook for 1 minute, then add the mixed peppers and cook for a further minute. Drain thoroughly.

Meanwhile prepare a moderate grill. Remove the rack and blend the oils and rosemary in the pan, seasoning with salt and pepper. Place the vegetables in the pan and toss to coat with the oils.

Grill for 8–10 minutes, tossing from time to time until the vegetables are tender and just tinged with brown. Remove from the pan with a slotted spoon and arrange on a heated serving platter.

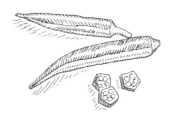

LEMON COOKED CELERIAC

SERVES 4

Celeriac has the flavour of celery and the texture of turnip. Its gnarled looking appearance resembles an ancient stone and some dexterity is required to peel this bulbous vegetable but it's well worth the effort. A fresh celeriac will seem heavy for its size and this is a good sign as when stale it becomes spongy, hollow and lighter in weight.

1 small lemon
1 × 450 g (1 lb) celeriac
salt
freshly ground black pepper

small knob butter
1 tablespoon fresh lemon thyme
leaves, chopped

Wash, dry and finely grate the lemon. Set the zest aside.

Remove the pith from the lemon, then segment and de-pip over a saucer to catch the juices.

Bring a large saucepan of salted water to the boil and add the lemon segments and juice.

Meanwhile scrub the celeriac in cold water. Peel on a chopping board with a stainless steel kitchen knife. Dice and add to the saucepan in batches.

Boil for about 5 minutes until just tender, then drain and season with pepper, and salt if necessary.

Turn into a heated dish, mix in the butter and thyme and sprinkle with the lemon zest.

LOW-FAT ROAST POTATOES

SERVES 4

Always use fresh oil for this recipe. Previously used frying oil will be more saturated due to the effect of high temperatures and residues of food particles from previously fried ingredients.

750 g (1½ lb) maincrop potatoes	2 tablespoons flour
e.g. King Edwards	2–3 tablespoons sunflower oil
salt	

Pre-heat the oven to gas mark 6, 400°F (200°C).

Peel the potatoes and cut into large even-sized pieces. Boil in salted water for 5 minutes. Drain thoroughly and spread out in a single layer.

Season the flour with salt and sift over the potatoes, turning them over to coat all sides. Shake off surplus flour.

Brush the oil all over the potatoes with a pastry brush. Place in a baking tin and bake for 30 minutes, turning the potatoes over half-way through cooking.

Raise the temperature to gas mark 8, 450°F (230°C) for 5 minutes to brown before serving.

MEDLEY OF GREEN BEANS

SERVES 4

A high fibre dish, low in calories and containing no saturated fat. Canned or frozen broad beans and frozen mangetout are acceptable, but fresh French beans do make a big difference.

225 g (8 oz) French beans, trimmed
100 g (4 oz) mangetout, trimmed
100 g (4 oz) shelled broad beans
1 medium onion, finely chopped
1 clove garlic, crushed
2 tablespoons olive oil

3 tomatoes, coarsely chopped
½ teaspoon thyme leaves
1 tablespoon chopped fresh parsley
2 bay leaves
salt
freshly ground black pepper

Cut the French beans into 2.5 cm (1 in) lengths and the mangetout lengthways. Cook in boiling salted water until crisp-tender.

Cook the broad beans in unsalted boiling water for about 15 minutes until soft.

Drain the vegetables and cool in a colander under cold running water. Shake off all excess water.

Combine the onion, garlic and oil in a large saucepan and cook until the onion is transparent. Add the tomato and herbs and cook for a few more minutes. Season with salt and pepper.

Remove the pan from the heat and stir in the green vegetables. Cover and leave for 2 hours for the flavours to mingle.

Re-heat when ready to serve and remove the bay leaves. Adjust the seasoning.

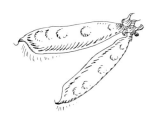

PAPRIKA POTATOES

SERVES 4

A useful recipe when boiled potatoes would not be quite exciting enough or would be too pale in colour. This also makes a nice change from frying or roasting.

450 g (1 lb) potatoes, peeled
1 onion, halved
40 g (1½ oz) butter or margarine

1½ tablespoons paprika
½ teaspoon salt

Cut the potatoes into 7.5 mm (⅜ in) slices.

Put the onion in a saucepan, half-fill with water and bring to the boil. Add the potato slices and cook until they are crisp-tender. Drain and discard the onion (which can be used up in soups).

Immediately put the butter or margarine in the saucepan and stir to melt in the residual heat. Stir in the paprika and salt.

Heat a moderate grill. Dip the potato slices in the paprika mixture, arrange in a single layer on the rack and grill until crisp, turning them over half-way through cooking.

PETITS POIS À LA FRANÇAISE

SERVES 4

Traditionally the recipe calls for large lettuce leaves which are poached above these little peas. No additional water is added. Nowadays fresh peas are hard to find and we all use the frozen kind which cook in a trice. Try my version.

15 g (½ oz) butter
300 g (11 oz) frozen petits pois
salt

freshly ground black pepper
2 Little Gem lettuces, coarsely
  shredded

Melt the butter in a large frying-pan and stir in the peas while still frozen. Season with salt and pepper.

Cover with the shredded lettuce and cover with a tight lid or foil. Cook over low heat for 10 minutes, shaking the pan occasionally. Check towards the end of cooking if you are apprehensive and concerned about drying out.

Serve hot, but left-overs are still tasty when cold.

PETITS POIS WITH CASHEW NUTS

SERVES 4

This recipe consists of whole peas and cashew nuts in a minted pea purée.

750 g (1½ lb) fresh shelled or frozen tiny peas
pinch sugar
salt

2 sprigs mint and 2 sprigs parsley tied together with white thread
25 g (1 oz) butter or margarine
50 g (2 oz) cashew nuts

Put the peas in a saucepan and add boiling water to cover. Add the sugar and season lightly with salt. Add the tied herbs. Cover with a lid and cook over moderate heat until the peas are tender.

Remove the herbs. Strain the peas reserving the liquid.

Return the liquid to the pan and simmer uncovered until reduced to one-third. Blend to a purée with half the peas.

Melt the butter in a frying-pan and sauté the cashew nuts until just beginning to change colour.

Return the purée, the remaining peas and the cashew nuts to the saucepan and re-heat gently.

119

PILAU RICE

SERVES 4

There is disagreement on when a pilau is a pilaff. In my understanding they are one and the same. Risotto, which is prepared in much the same way, should use Piedmont Italian rice which is shorter than the American long grain and thicker than the Indian Basmati. This is often known as Patna and is marketed as such in the UK. Indian rices should be soaked before cooking. Easy-cook rice can usually be cooked straight from the packet.

25 g (1 oz) butter or margarine	salt
1 small onion, finely chopped	freshly ground black pepper
175 g (6 oz) easy-cook long grain rice	2 bay leaves
450 ml (¾ pint) hot stock	

Melt half of the butter in a large saucepan, stir in the onion, cover with a tightly fitting lid and cook over low heat, shaking the pan from time to time until the onion is tender.

Mix in the rice, replace the lid and cook for 1–2 minutes.

Bring the stock to the boil and pour into the rice, adding about ½ teaspoon salt and a generous shake of pepper. Add the bay leaves and cook covered over moderate heat for about 15 minutes.

Test a grain of rice to see if it is nearly cooked when most of the liquid should have been absorbed. Cook if necessary for a few more minutes.

Remove the bay leaves, adjust the seasoning and fork in the remaining butter if wished.

POMMES AMANDINE

SERVES 4

These croquette potatoes are out of this world and bear no relation to the commercially frozen kind. They are soft and rich tasting due to the ground almonds which, in addition, make them nutritionally more valuable. If preferred they will roast nicely in a little oil in a hot oven which should not take over-long as they are already cooked.

750 g (1½ lb) baking potatoes, peeled
25 g (1 oz) butter or margarine
25 g (1 oz) ground almonds
2 eggs, beaten

salt
freshly ground black pepper
75–100 g (3–4 oz) chopped almonds
oil for frying

Cut up the potatoes and cook in boiling salted water until tender.

Drain thoroughly and mash in the butter, ground almonds and sufficient egg to bind. Season to taste with salt and pepper.

Leave until cool enough to handle and shape into 12 'thick sausages'. Brush with the remaining egg and coat with the chopped almonds and refrigerate in a single layer for 30 minutes to firm.

Fry in 2 cm (1 in) hot oil for a few minutes, turning them over after 30 seconds to prevent them becoming misshapen. Reduce the heat if the almonds become brown too quickly, to allow the centres to heat thoroughly.

RATATOUILLE

SERVES 4

A watery ratatouille is not a ratatouille at all, but a miserable vegetable casserole. If necessary, continue cooking gently until most of the spare liquid has evaporated, leaving a concentrated flavoursome sauce. When fresh tomatoes are expensive substitute their perfectly respectable canned cousins.

2 large onions
2 cloves garlic
3 tablespoons sunflower oil
1 teaspoon walnut oil
2 red peppers, de-seeded and sliced
  into thin rings
1 green pepper, de-seeded and sliced
  into thin rings
1 medium aubergine, cut into small
  pieces

450 g (1 lb) ripe tomatoes, skinned
  or 1 equivalent can
3 small courgettes, topped, tailed
  and finely sliced
salt
freshly ground black pepper
2 teaspoons chopped fresh basil leaves

Slice one onion thinly and chop the other. Skin and thinly slice the garlic. Sauté both in the oils in a heavy-based saucepan until beginning to colour slightly.

Add the peppers and aubergine and cook gently for 10 minutes, stirring from time to time to prevent sticking.

Add the tomatoes and courgettes, cover with the lid and continue cooking for 15 minutes.

Season with salt and pepper and add the basil.

Reduce to a very low heat and cook uncovered for 25–30 minutes or until most of the liquid has evaporated. Adjust the seasoning and serve hot, cold or re-heated when required.

RED PEPPER COMPÔTE

SERVES 4

Cooked this way the red peppers retain their glorious colour. When grilling don't worry if the skins blacken in places as this all comes away when they are peeled. They are likely to collapse after coring but this will not affect the finished dish either.

4 red peppers	2 tablespoons sunflower oil
2 small lovage leaves, finely scissored	¼ teaspoon salt
freshly ground black pepper	3 spring onions, finely chopped
2 tablespoons red wine vinegar	1 tablespoon tomato purée

Place the peppers under a moderate grill, turning them during cooking so that all surfaces are blistered.

Peel carefully as the peppers will be very hot and remove the cores and seeds. Slice thinly.

Combine all the ingredients in a frying-pan, add 6 tablespoons water and cover tightly with a lid or foil and cook over low heat until the peppers are tender.

Serve in a heated covered dish.

RICE PIMENTO CASTLES

SERVES 4

Dariole moulds are individual turret-shaped tins mostly used for baking Madeleines. Ramekin dishes, although shorter, also produce a pretty effect.

227 g (8 oz) can of pimentos, drained
1 green chilli
25 g (1 oz) butter or margarine

1 small onion, finely chopped
350 g (12 oz) cooked long grain rice
garlic salt

Dice the pimientos and set aside. Cut the green chilli in half vertically and discard the seeds. Slice thinly.

Melt the butter or margarine in a saucepan and fry the sliced chilli and onion until soft. Mix in the diced pimento and rice, and season to taste with garlic salt.

Pack the mixture tightly into individual castle or dariole moulds and cover each with a foil lid. Place in a frying-pan. Pour water into the pan to reach half-way up the moulds and cook over moderate heat for 10 minutes to thoroughly heat.

Invert two moulds on to one side of each plate before serving the other dishes, carefully removing the moulds to reveal the rice pimento castles.

RICE AND LENTIL COMPÔTE

SERVES 4

Rice and lentils complement one another in a vegetarian diet. This recipe is suitable as a side vegetable, whenever needed, to improve the balance of the nutrients in a meal.

75 g (3 oz) long grain rice
75 g (3 oz) continental lentils
salt
1 beef tomato, skinned and sieved

2 leaves fresh coriander,
 finely scissored
freshly ground black pepper

Rinse the rice and lentils, put them in a saucepan and add 450 ml (¾ pint) boiling water and ½ teaspoon salt. Bring back to the boil, then reduce the heat and simmer for 15 minutes until tender. Add extra boiling water towards the end of cooking if needed.

Drain in a colander and pour extra boiling water through to separate the grains.

Mix with the sieved tomato and coriander and season to taste with salt and pepper.

Serve hot or cold.

ROAST PUMPKIN

SERVES 4

Pumpkin is an inexpensive vegetable and really comes into its own at Hallowe'en. It is an interesting autumn vegetable and after removing the flesh, it can be made into a decorative party lantern. Pumpkin is used widely in America for the dessert Pumpkin Pie and I would suggest that you try this out if your purchased pumpkin proves to be too large. Roast pumpkin does not crispen in the same way as roast potatoes, always remaining soft. Remove from the tin with a fish slice.

750 g (1½ lb) wedge of pumpkin	salt
1 tablespoon plain flour	3 tablespoons vegetable oil
½ teaspoon ground allspice	

Pre-heat the oven to gas mark 7, 425°F (220°C).

Pare away the pumpkin peel, remove and discard the pulp and seeds. Cut into 4–6 boat shaped slices.

Mix the flour, allspice, and about ½ teaspoon salt together and sift over the pumpkin through a clean sieve.

Put the oil in a shallow roasting tin and heat in the oven for 3–5 minutes until very hot.

Using kitchen tongs place the pumpkin slices in the tin in a single layer. Bake for 15 minutes, then carefully reverse the slices and bake for a further 10 minutes. Drain on kitchen paper and serve hot.

SAFFRON RICE

SERVES 4–5

Saffron is understandably expensive, coming from the stamen of the crocus and 60,000 are needed to produce 450 g (1 lb). Only a few strands are needed to introduce a delicate flavour and colour which will be more intense when steeped in a little water for several hours. In spicy cookery turmeric can be substituted, as its characteristic flavour will be masked. Easy-cook (pre-fluffed) rice is cooked in twice its volume of liquid and the grains remain separate.

6 strands saffron, crumbled
225 g (8 oz) easy-cook long grain rice
1 teaspoon salt
2 tablespoons pine kernels, chopped

1 tablespoon shelled pistachio nuts, skinned and chopped
2 tablespoons sultanas
freshly ground black pepper

Put 550 ml (18 fl oz) water in a saucepan and stir in the saffron. Leave for 30 minutes.

Stir in the rice, salt, pine kernels, pistachios, sultanas and add pepper to taste. Bring to the boil, then reduce the heat, cover and cook gently for 15 minutes until the rice is just tender and nearly all of the liquid has been absorbed.

Remove from the heat and leave tightly covered for 5 minutes. Fluff up with a fork to separate the grains.

SAVOY CABBAGE AND TOMATO FRICASSÉE

SERVES 4

The Savoy cabbage has light green leaves which are prominently veined. A fresh cabbage should have tightly packed inside leaves and should feel heavy in relation to its size.

1 small Savoy cabbage
25 g (1 oz) butter or margarine
salt
freshly ground black pepper

2 teaspoons scissored fresh basil leaves
225 g (½ lb) tomatoes, chopped
2 tablespoons orange juice

126

Wash and cut the cabbage into quarters. Shred finely, discarding the tough core and outer leaves.

Melt the butter or margarine in a saucepan and stir in the cabbage. Season with salt and pepper and cook covered for 2–3 minutes until some liquid escapes from the cabbage.

Add the remaining ingredients and cook without covering until the cabbage is crisp-tender and most of the liquid has evaporated.

SPICY SPINACH

SERVES 4–5

Fresh spinach should be the first choice in this recipe, as canned or frozen chopped spinach is not really suitable because it alters the taste. However, frozen leaf spinach can be substituted.

4–6 cardamom pods	1 kg (2 lb) fresh spinach
7 g (¼ oz) butter or margarine	salt
¼ teaspoon mustard seeds	freshly ground black pepper

Open the cardamom pods and take out the seeds.

Melt the butter in a small pan and lightly fry the cardamom and mustard seeds until they pop. Drain and set aside.

Wash the fresh spinach in several changes of cold water, drain and remove the tough stems. Cook in a few tablespoons of water over moderate heat in a tightly lidded pan until tender. Shake the pan from time to time during cooking to prevent sticking.

Drain thoroughly and coarsely chop the spinach. Return to the pan to stir in the seeds, season with salt and pepper and heat thoroughly, stirring continuously.

SWEDE AND CARROT PURÉE

SERVES 4

Swede is not the easiest of vegetables to peel. Strong hands and a non-slip chopping board are needed. Remove a slice from both ends, then peel vertically with a sharp knife. Swede can be cooked whole in the microwave or pressure cooker but, due to its density, it would take a very long time to cook in a saucepan on the hob.

450 g (1 lb) swede, peeled and cubed
2 medium carrots, peeled and diced
salt

freshly ground black pepper
pinch ground allspice
4 tablespoons single cream

Cook the swede and carrots in boiling salted water until soft. Drain, reserving the liquid.

Season vegetables with salt and pepper to taste and add the allspice. Blend in the food processor or mash thoroughly and add sufficient reserved liquid to thin to a purée.

Return the purée to the saucepan and cook over the lowest possible heat, stirring continuously until thoroughly reheated.

Stir in the cream and serve at once.

TOUJOURS CAULIFLOWER

◆ *Very tasty!*

SERVES 4

In most recipes the difference in taste between the frozen and fresh florets is markedly noticeable. In this recipe, since the vegetable is baked after steaming, the question of which to buy does not arise. Either will do and in any case the frozen is an excellent stand-by.

1 kg (2 lb) cauliflower florets
4 tablespoons grated Parmesan cheese
2 tablespoons fresh breadcrumbs
  (either brown or white)
50 g (2 oz) butter or margarine

200 ml (7 fl oz) creamy milk
salt
freshly ground black pepper
2 tablespoons freshly chopped parsley

Pre-heat the oven to gas mark 5, 375°F (190°C).

Cook the cauliflower in a minimum of boiling water until crisp-tender. Remove half the cauliflower with a slotted spoon and arrange in a border in a shallow oven-proof dish.

Sprinkle with the Parmesan and breadcrumbs and dot with half of the butter or margarine. Bake for 20–25 minutes until brown on top.

Meanwhile continue cooking the remaining cauliflower in the saucepan until soft.

Drain thoroughly, then purée with the milk and the rest of the butter. Season to taste with salt and pepper. Return to the saucepan and heat thoroughly. Stir in the parsley.

Pour the purée into the centre of the baked cauliflower and serve hot.

Companion Sauces

CREAMY HOLLANDAISE SAUCE

MAKES 300 ML (½ PINT)

Cook this sauce in a double saucepan or bowl set over a pan of simmering water. Whisk continuously and make sure that the water does not touch the bottom of the bowl or curdling may occur. If preferred cook the sauce by microwave. Use a low setting and beat every 15 seconds.

2 eggs plus 1 yolk
2 tablespoons fresh lemon juice
3 tablespoons Greek-style yogurt
salt

freshly ground black pepper
100 g (4 oz) polyunsaturated
  margarine

Beat the eggs, extra yolk, lemon juice and yogurt together and season with salt and pepper.

Melt the margarine in a double saucepan or bowl set over simmering water, avoiding the direct heat.

Add the egg mixture all at once and beat with a whisk until blended. Continue cooking, whisking vigorously until the sauce is the consistency of double cream.

Remove from the heat and continue whisking until cool.

CIDER GRAVY

MAKES 300 ML (½ PINT)

The joy of this gravy is that it contains no cholesterol. Gravies made purely with powder or granules have little depth of taste unless meat juices are added. This, of course, reduces their value to vegetarians.

350 ml (12 fl oz) strong dry cider
20 g (¾ oz) cornflour
25 g (1 oz) polyunsaturated margarine
¼ onion stock cube

pinch of bay leaf powder
salt
freshly ground black pepper

Pour the cider and 150 ml (¼ pint) water into a medium saucepan. Blend in the cornflour, then add the margarine.

Put the pan over moderate heat and bring to the boil, whisking continuously.

Crumble in the stock cube, add the bay leaf powder and season with salt and pepper. Reduce to minimum heat and cook gently for 5 minutes, stirring from time to time. Strain into a jug.

ESPAGNOLE SAUCE

MAKES 550 ML (18 FL OZ)

Cutlets, terrines, burgers and croquettes, unless served with a puréed vegetable, may tend to be on the dry side. This invaluable sauce is remarkably easy to make. Prepare a double quantity and freeze it if you wish, then use the microwave for thawing and heating if you have one.

2 tablespoons vegetable oil
1 medium onion, finely sliced
25 g (1 oz) flour
100 g (4 oz) flat mushrooms,
 finely chopped
1 tablespoon tomato purée

1 stock cube
salt
freshly ground black pepper
2 bay leaves
150 ml (¼ pint) medium red wine

Heat the oil in a large frying-pan and fry the onion until brown.

Stir in the flour and cook over moderate heat, stirring frequently until this too is light brown.

Add the mushrooms, 450 ml (¾ pint) hot water, the tomato purée and crumble in the stock cube. Stir over moderate heat until the liquid thickens. Season with salt and pepper and add the bay leaves.

Raise the heat and simmer uncovered for 10 minutes, stirring from time to time to prevent sticking, then add most of the wine and continue cooking for about 5 minutes.

Remove the bay leaves and purée the mixture in a food processor. Return it to the pan, add the remaining wine and re-heat as required. If not needed immediately, replace the bay leaves and remove them when you are ready to serve.

MUSTARD SAUCE

SERVES 4–6

Thirty seconds to mix plus ten minutes to bring out the flavour is all that is needed for this powerful sauce. Only a little is needed to perk up blander dishes.

1 tablespoon mustard powder	pepper
pinch of salt	4 tablespoons single cream
¼ teaspoon freshly ground black	

Blend the mustard powder, salt and pepper with the cream. Cover and leave for 10 minutes.

If required the sauce will keep refrigerated for up to 8 hours.

PESTO

MAKES 300 ML (½ PINT)

Pesto is a traditional Italian sauce specifically for pasta and gnocchi. Its main ingredient is basil which must be fresh. Basil can be grown in the garden or in a pot on the window ledge. Like other popular herbs, ready grown basil is obtainable from most supermarkets and is usually located near the vegetable section. No cooking is required in this liquidiser recipe. Store for a short time in a screw top jar in the refrigerator.

120 ml (4 fl oz) olive oil	¼ teaspoon salt
50 g (2 oz) pine kernels	½ teaspoon freshly ground black
1 clove garlic, peeled	pepper
75 g (3 oz) fresh basil leaves	50 g (2 oz) grated Parmesan cheese

Blend the ingredients except the Parmesan in a liquidiser until smooth.
Add the Parmesan and whizz briefly.

QUICK TOMATO SAUCE

MAKES 450 ML (¾ PINT)

Cook this sauce in an uncovered pan and be prepared for it to spatter. A perforated straining lid will help to reduce this. For a perfect finish, purée the sauce thoroughly.

400 g (14 oz) can chopped tomatoes
  with garlic and herbs
4 tablespoons olive oil

generous squeeze of fresh lemon juice
salt
freshly ground black pepper

Mix the tomatoes, oil and lemon juice in a saucepan, bring to the boil, reduce the heat and cook gently for 10 minutes or until reduced slightly.

Purée in the food processor. Re-heat and season to taste.

SAGE AND ONION SAUCE

MAKES 400 ML (14 FL OZ)

This sauce is suitable to serve with drier savoury puddings and pastry to help moisten the palate.

450 g (1 lb) onions, thinly sliced
600 ml (1 pint) creamy milk
4 sage leaves
salt

freshly ground black pepper
2 tablespoons double cream or
  Greek-style yogurt

Combine the onions, milk and sage leaves in a large saucepan, bring to the boil, then reduce the heat and simmer until tender. Stir occasionally to prevent a skin from forming.

Strain the liquid into another saucepan, reserving the onions and sage. Simmer, stirring occasionally, until reduced by one-third.

Purée the onions and sage in the food processor, then stir into the reserved liquid.

Re-heat, season to taste with salt and pepper and stir in the cream or yogurt.

133

SOURED CREAM GRAVY

MAKES 200 ML (7 FL OZ)

A smooth full-flavoured gravy with a pink-brown colour which is very low in cholesterol. Serve with main dishes or any vegetables that have been boiled or steamed.

1 tablespoon sesame seed oil
1 tablespoon sunflower oil
2 tablespoons plain flour
6 tablespoons red wine
200 ml (7 fl oz) vegetable stock
1 thin slice of onion

3 slices celery
salt
freshly ground black pepper
4 tablespoons soured cream or
   Greek-style yogurt

Blend the oils and flour in a small saucepan and cook over moderate heat, stirring continuously until a rich brown colour.

Remove the pan from the heat and gradually blend in the wine and stock. Add the onion and celery. Cook over moderate heat, stirring continuously until boiled, then reduce the heat to minimum and continue cooking for 7–10 minutes to develop the flavour.

Strain into another saucepan, season to taste with salt and pepper, bring back to the boil, then switch off the heat and stir in the soured cream or yogurt.

Do not re-heat or the gravy may curdle. To keep hot, cover the jug of gravy and stand it in a bowl of near boiling water. If the jug is made of a suitable material, the gravy could be kept hot in the microwave on 10 per cent of full power.

TARRAGON HOLLANDAISE SAUCE

MAKES 350 ML (12 FL OZ)

Recipes for Hollandaise sauce abound and I felt that it would be nice to have an alternative to the basic recipe. Here is a quick blender one for the cook in a hurry. It is wonderfully light and so simple to make.

2 eggs
1 tablespoon fresh lemon juice
4–6 tarragon leaves
100 g (4 oz) polyunsaturated

margarine
salt
freshly ground black pepper

Break the eggs into the blender, add 1 tablespoon warm water, the lemon juice and tarragon and whizz for 1 minute until light and frothy.

Melt the margarine in a small saucepan over the lowest heat until melted but not transparent.

Add the egg mixture all at once and cook still over lowest heat, stirring vigorously and constantly for 30 seconds only. Do not overheat or curdling will occur which shows itself as lumps on the bottom of the mixture. Should this happen, immediately return the sauce to the blender and whizz for 30 seconds.

Season with salt and pepper and serve warm.

WARM LEMON VINAIGRETTE

SERVES 4

Fresh lemon refreshes the palate and stimulates the salivary juices. Bottled lemon juice will not do in this recipe. This recipe only makes about 5 tablespoons sauce but the quantities can be doubled or trebled. Mix in advance if desired but do not heat until required.

2 tablespoons freshly squeezed
  lemon juice
1½ tablespoons sunflower oil
½ tablespoon walnut oil
½ teaspoon salt

½ teaspoon freshly ground black
  pepper
½ teaspoon sugar
½ teaspoon made English mustard

Combine all the ingredients in a screw top jar and shake thoroughly. Remove the lid and stand the jar on a rack in a saucepan.

Add warm water to reach half-way up the outside of the jar, then heat until the water is very hot but not boiling or the water will spatter into the vinaigrette.

Remove from the heat, stir the sauce well, then carefully remove it with oven-gloves.

Alternatively place the unlidded jar in the microwave and heat for 20 seconds. Stir before serving.

SIDE SALADS AND ACCOMPANIMENTS

The art of preparing inspired side salads depends first and foremost on the availability of dew-fresh salad ingredients, and secondly on the choice and combination of these.

Cucumbers and radishes must be firm and not spongy when squeezed, and lettuce should have crisp leaves with bright true colours and no sign of wilt.

Prepare salads as close to the time of serving as possible and, unless instructed otherwise, mix in dressings only just before serving. Leaves should be torn or sliced with a stainless steel knife, and handled as little as possible to avoid bruising.

Side salads need not consist of vegetables alone. Fruit, nuts, seeds, cheese, eggs, rice, pasta and beans represent only some of the numerous additions worthy of inclusion.

The recipes given in this chapter are extra ones which make tasty dishes in their own right, and will accompany both hot and cold meals.

Side Salads

AVOCADO SALAD

SERVES 4

They say that avocados can be ripened in the airing cupboard. This is true if they are a little too firm, but if they are rock hard the chances are that they will go bad before they ripen. Try to avoid microwave advice to pop them in for half a minute – the result is cooking and not thawing and the taste is indescribable!

2 boxes cress
4 tablespoons mayonnaise
1 tablespoon fresh lemon juice
2–3 spring onions, trimmed and
  finely sliced

2 tablespoons cooked red kidney beans
salt
freshly ground black pepper
2 ripe avocados e.g. the Carmel
  variety

Cut the cress away from the soil and wash in a strainer. Spin in a salad shaker or pat dry between kitchen paper. Arrange on a serving platter.

Mix the mayonnaise, lemon juice, onions and kidney beans and season with salt and pepper.

Halve the avocados lengthwise and squeeze gently to remove the stones. Using a grapefruit knife separate the flesh from the skin and lift out the avocados carefully (alternatively hold carefully in the palm of one hand and remove the peel).

Place on the bed of cress and spoon the kidney bean filling into the cavities.

CUCUMBER RAITA

SERVES 4

Generally served as a curry accompaniment, cucumber raita goes well with any spicy hot main course. It gives a refreshing, cooling effect to the palate.

1 small onion
½ large cucumber
½ teaspoon cumin seeds
225 ml (8 fl oz) plain yogurt

½ teaspoon salt
½ teaspoon freshly ground black
  pepper

Finely slice the onion, peel and dice the cucumber.

Put the cumin seeds on to a piece of foil and grill for 30 seconds until the seeds pop. Leave to cool.

Beat the yogurt, cumin, salt and pepper together.

Fold in the onion and cucumber and chill in the refrigerator for 2 hours before serving.

CURRIED EGG SALAD

SERVES 4

The only sure way of shelling hard-boiled eggs without damage is to do it while they are hot, otherwise it is difficult to get off all the shell without spoiling the smooth surface of the white. To be successful in this, start peeling at the wider end of the egg.

4 eggs
2 tablespoons mayonnaise
1 teaspoon garam masala
pinch chilli powder
salt
generous shake of freshly ground black
  pepper

8 small coriander leaves
4 tablespoons Greek-style yogurt
½ teaspoon grated ginger root
2 shallots, finely chopped
1 tablespoon sultanas, chopped
about ½ iceberg lettuce, coarsely
  shredded

Put the eggs in a saucepan of cold, lightly salted water, bring to the boil and simmer for 10 minutes.

Remove the eggs and plunge them into cold water to cool the shells only. Tap on a hard surface to crack the shells before unpeeling. Leave to cool.

Halve eggs lengthways with a sharp stainless steel knife. Scoop out the yolks and mash with the mayonnaise, garam masala, chilli powder and salt and pepper to taste.

Fill the egg-whites with the mixture, rounding the tops. Ridge with a fork. Decorate with coriander leaves.

Mix the yogurt, ginger root, shallots and sultanas together.

Add the lettuce and toss well, then arrange on a serving platter and nestle the stuffed eggs on top.

EGG AND CUCUMBER SALAD

SERVES 4

Greek-style yogurt is creamy, but read the list of ingredients as some kinds have added cream which you may feel is unnecessary.

4 tablespoons Greek-style yogurt
2 tablespoons olive oil
½ tablespoon fresh lemon juice
pinch ground cinnamon
salt
freshly ground black pepper
¼ small cucumber, diced
4 eggs, hard-boiled and thinly sliced
half a box of cress, rinsed
¼ teaspoon cayenne pepper

Blend the yogurt, oil, lemon juice, cinnamon and salt and black pepper to taste. Spread a thin layer in the bottom of a shallow serving dish.

Cover with the cucumber, followed by a layer of dressing, and a quarter of the egg. Repeat the layers finishing with egg.

Snip the cress with scissors over the top and dust with the cayenne pepper.

ENDIVE AND RADISH SALAD

SERVES 4

The darker outside endive leaves are slightly bitter and, although acceptable in salads, are really delicious when cooked as a vegetable. The macaroni must be completely dry before frying to eliminate spattering.

100 g (4 oz) wholewheat macaroni
½ endive, light green part only
1 bunch large radishes, trimmed
1 tablespoon walnut oil

4 tablespoons olive oil
2 tablespoons mayonnaise
garlic salt
freshly ground black pepper

Cook the macaroni in boiling salted water adding a teaspoon of oil to prevent sticking. Rinse under cold water before draining. Set aside.

Separate the endive leaves and cut into sprigs, thinly slice the radishes and soak together in ice cold water for 30 minutes.

Heat the oils together in a small saucepan and fry the macaroni a few pieces at a time until golden brown. Remove with a slotted spoon and drain on kitchen paper.

Season the mayonnaise with garlic salt and pepper to taste.

Drain the endive and radishes, pat or spin dry, then add the mayonnaise and toss well. Mix in the macaroni croûtons. Turn into a salad bowl and serve freshly prepared.

FETA AND BLACK OLIVE SALAD

SERVES 4

Feta is a salty cheese as are some black olives, especially those which are packed with salt alone rather than in brine. A short soak in cold water helps to reduce their saltiness.

12 black olives, stoned
2 teaspoons fresh lemon juice
freshly ground black pepper
shake of cayenne pepper

about 6 Cos lettuce leaves
200 g (7 oz) Feta cheese, diced
12 slender spring onions, trimmed
2 mint leaves, finely scissored

Finely chop half of the olives. Mix with the lemon juice and season with the black and cayenne peppers. Transfer to a wooden salad bowl.

Add the lettuce torn into pieces and toss together.

Top with the Feta, remaining whole olives and spring onions and scatter with the mint.

GRATED CARROT AND PINEAPPLE SALAD

SERVES 4

The spice star anise is now displayed in the spice sections of most shops. The flavour is similar to aniseed and I have used it in this salad to reduce the sweetness of the pineapple.

1 thin slice of day-old white bread	1 star anise, finely crushed
2 tablespoons sunflower oil	1 teaspoon walnut oil
225 g (8 oz) can pineapple pieces	salt
in natural juice	3 medium carrots

Remove the crusts and cut the bread into tiny dice.

Heat the sunflower oil in a frying-pan and when very hot, fry the diced bread, turning it over frequently until golden on all sides. Remove and drain on kitchen paper. Set aside until cool.

Strain the pineapple juice into a small saucepan and stir in the star anise. Simmer for a few minutes until only 2 tablespoons of the juice remain. Leave to cool.

Strain into a salad bowl, discard the star anise, add the walnut oil and season lightly with salt.

Peel and grate the carrots into the juice. Stir in the pineapple pieces and fold in the diced fried bread just before serving.

HOT BEETROOT SALAD

SERVES 4

Small raw beetroot can be cooked so easily in the microwave. Just give them a quick wash but do not peel or remove the stalks. Fit the beetroot comfortably into a bowl and add sufficient boiling water to reach half-way up the sides. Cover with a vented lid or well pricked cling film and cook on full power for 5–8 minutes, turning the beetroot over half-way through. Otherwise cook the beetroot in a saucepan of water or use ready-cooked beetroot that isn't preserved in vinegar.

4 small cooked beetroot
15 g (½ oz) butter or margarine
175 g (6 oz) can evaporated milk
4 tablespoons stock

3 tablespoons chopped fresh parsley
1 tablespoon chopped fresh chives
salt
freshly ground black pepper

Pre-heat the oven to gas mark 4, 350°F (180°C).

Place the beetroot in a casserole dish, add 1 tablespoon of water, cover with the lid and heat in the oven for 15 minutes.

Meanwhile combine the butter or margarine, milk and stock in a heavy-based saucepan and cook over moderate heat, stirring to prevent a skin from forming, until reduced to the consistency of a coating sauce.

Stir in the parsley and chives, season with salt and pepper and cook for 3 more minutes.

Pour the hot sauce over the beetroot and serve at once.

INSALATA PAESE

SERVES 4

A piquant salad attractive in both taste and appearance.

175 g (6 oz) cooked or canned
  borlotti beans, drained
6 tomatoes, thickly sliced
salt
freshly ground black pepper
4 tablespoons red wine
4 spring onions, trimmed and
  thinly sliced

1 small head chicory, sliced
1 medium green pepper, de-seeded
  and cut into rings
6 stuffed green olives
8 stoned black olives
3 tablespoons fromage frais
generous dash of Tabasco sauce

Put the beans in a salad bowl, cover with the tomatoes and season with salt and pepper. Spoon over the wine and set aside for 30 minutes.

Cover with the onions, chicory and green pepper rings and top with the olives arranged in overlapping alternate colours.

Spoon over the fromage frais and finish with a few shakes of Tabasco.

LEMON DRESSED GREEN SALAD

SERVES 4

The endive has attractive fern-shaped leaves. The outside darker leaves can be somewhat bitter but the paler green heart has a lovely nutty flavour. Chinese leaves, sometimes called Bok Choy, endive and celery make a fine salad. The tasty dressing will separate unless beaten just before use. I think it is a pity to spoil the excellent flavour but if preferred, an added teaspoon of mayonnaise will act as a stabiliser.

2 sticks celery
1 endive heart
4–6 Chinese leaves
1 tablespoon fresh lemon juice
3 tablespoons sunflower oil

1 tablespoon Greek-style yogurt
pinch sugar
salt
freshly ground black pepper
1 teaspoon chopped fresh dill weed

Quarter the celery sticks, then slice lengthwise into strips. Soak in ice cold water in the refrigerator for 1–2 hours until the celery curls. Drain thoroughly.

Wash and thoroughly drain the endive, and separate into sprigs.

Remove the tough stalks and shred the Chinese leaves.

Blend the lemon juice, oil, yogurt and sugar together in a salad bowl. Season with salt and pepper.

Add the endive, Chinese leaves and celery curls and toss to mix. Scatter with the dill weed.

MINTED TOMATO SALAD

◆

SERVES 4

So many salads consist of sliced vegetables that this makes a refreshing change. The tomatoes are served whole having absorbed the flavour of the marinade.

1 tablespoon medium white wine
1 tablespoon red wine vinegar
3 tablespoons sunflower oil
1 tablespoon olive oil

salt
freshly ground black pepper
1 tablespoon chopped fresh mint
275 g (10 oz) baby tomatoes

Combine the wine, vinegar and oils in a salad bowl and season with salt and pepper. Stir in half of the mint.

Prick the tomatoes thoroughly with a fine skewer and add to the bowl. Refrigerate for 1–2 hours, turning the tomatoes from time to time.

Sprinkle with the remaining mint just before serving.

PEANUT AND GEM LETTUCE SALAD

◆

SERVES 4

The Gem is an economical lettuce since there are few or no leaves that have to be thrown away. Peanuts are high in protein and fat and so improve the nutritional value of the salad.

50 g (2 oz) shelled peanuts
2½ tablespoons fresh lemon juice
salt and pepper

2 Little Gem lettuces
10 fresh chives, finely scissored

Spread the peanuts in a grill pan and brown under the grill until the skins crispen. Spoon on to a clean teacloth, gather up the sides and rub briskly to remove the skins.

Blend the peanuts in a food processor with the lemon juice and season to taste. Blend in 5 second spurts until smooth.

Quarter, then coarsely shred the lettuces crosswise. Put in a salad bowl, add the peanut paste and toss to mix. Sprinkle with the chives.

PINK GRAPEFRUIT AND WATERCRESS SALAD

◆

SERVES 4

Pink grapefruit are less sharp than the more common, yellow-fleshed kind. Although the skin colour is not much different, the flesh has an attractive pink tinge and a less pungent flavour.

1 pink grapefruit
1 large bunch watercress, washed
 and trimmed
50 g (2 oz) Gouda cheese, grated
4 tablespoons natural yogurt

1 teaspoon tomato purée
pinch of sugar
salt
freshly ground black pepper

Peel the grapefruit, separate the segments and remove the pith, skin and pips over a plate to catch the juice. Cut up the flesh, transfer to a salad bowl and add the watercress and half of the cheese.

Mix the juice, yogurt, tomato purée and sugar in a jug and season with salt and pepper.

Pour the dressing over the salad, toss and refrigerate for 15 minutes. Top with the remaining cheese just before serving.

RICE AND MANGETOUT SALAD

◆

SERVES 4

Brown rice takes longer to cook than white because the husks are not removed. Although primarily devised as a cold salad the dish is equally palatable and attractive served hot as a side vegetable.

175 g (6 oz) brown long grain rice
175 g (6 oz) mangetout
6–8 mint leaves, finely scissored
2 teaspoons fresh lemon juice

1 teaspoon olive oil
1 teaspoon hazelnut oil
salt
freshly ground black pepper

Cook the rice according to the directions on the packet.

While the rice is cooking, trim the mangetout and thinly slice diagonally. Add to the rice during the final 3 minutes of cooking to crisp-cook. Drain thoroughly.

Mix in the mint, lemon juice and oils whilst hot, and season with salt and pepper after cooling. Adjust seasoning and fork up before serving.

TABBOULEH

SERVES 4–5

Tabbouleh is a Lebanese salad whose main ingredient is bulgar which is a variety of cracked wheat. Other dishes in this book include bulgar so that the purchase of a packet will not mean that the rest is wasted. Bulgar is so easy to prepare and does make a nice change from pasta and rice.

225 g (8 oz) bulgar (cracked wheat)
1 onion, finely chopped
3 tomatoes, skinned and coarsely
  chopped
6 tablespoons chopped fresh parsley
1 tablespoon fresh mint, finely
  scissored
juice of 2 lemons

3 tablespoons olive oil
5 tablespoons sunflower oil
salt
freshly ground black pepper

Garnish ....
12 black olives (optional)

Put the bulgar in a bowl and add 600 ml (1 pint) boiling water. Stir and leave for 30 minutes.

Drain through a sieve until the mixture stops dripping. Cover and refrigerate for an hour.

Meanwhile combine the onion, tomatoes, parsley and mint in a large salad bowl and thoroughly mix in the lemon juice and oils. Season with the salt and pepper.

Fold in the bulgar in batches. Adjust the seasoning and garnish with black olives if desired.

THREE-LETTUCE SALAD

SERVES 4

Naturally a combination salad of three lettuces would be enough for a dozen or more people. If you are in the habit of eating a lot of salad and adventurous enough to try different varieties, you will be able to use up the surplus within a few days. Provided lettuce is spun dry after washing and kept in a ventilated box rather than a plastic bag, it will stay crisp for up to 5 days.

½ Lollo Rosso
¼ Webb's lettuce
1 small Radicchio

Dressing ....
1 clove garlic, peeled and crushed
5 tablespoons olive oil

½ teaspoon mustard powder
1 tablespoon fresh lemon juice
1 teaspoon grated lemon rind
1 tablespoon chopped fresh parsley
salt
freshly ground black pepper

Wash and thoroughly dry the lettuce leaves and arrange in a salad bowl, lining the bowl with the purple frilly Lollo Rosso, then a layer of Webb's lettuce and arrange the red Radicchio in the centre.

Shake the dressing ingredients together in a screw-top jar and pour over the lettuce. Toss after taking the bowl to the table.

WATERCRESS, PEAR AND
GREEN PEPPERCORN SALAD

SERVES 4

All sorts of unusual whole spices are appearing in larger grocers and supermarkets, many of which come from far away places. Until recently, green peppercorns have been sold bottled in brine, but at last they are obtainable in strings like tiny jade beads. They will keep in the refrigerator for a few days.

2 bunches watercress
1 juicy pear (William or similar)
16 green peppercorns, crushed

2 teaspoons unsweetened apple juice
2 teaspoons walnut oil

Trim away any coarse stems and cut the watercress into bite-size lengths.
   Remove the stalk from the pear, quarter, core and slice thinly.
   Combine the peppercorns, apple juice and oil in a salad bowl.
   Mix in the watercress and pear and toss thoroughly. Serve fresh.

Accompaniments

FLOUR TORTILLAS

MAKES ABOUT 12

Serve these with Mexican dishes or in place of pitta bread or chapattis. Flour tortillas can be stored in the freezer, interleaved with greaseproof or waxed paper and wrapped in a double layer of foil.

175 g (6 oz) plain flour   1 teaspoon salt
50 g (2 oz) wholemeal flour   50 g (2 oz) white vegetable fat

Mix the flours and salt in a mixing bowl. Rub in the fat, then gradually add 8–10 tablespoons of warm water and knead to a soft dough. Wrap in buttered foil and leave for 30 minutes.

Divide the dough into 10 or 12 pieces and shape into balls with floured hands. Roll each out to a thin round on plenty of flour, using an upturned plate to trim round to attain an even shape.

Cook the tortillas one at a time in a lightly floured frying-pan over moderate heat for 25–50 seconds on each side or until brown patches appear dusting the pan with flour each time.

Stack the pancakes in a dry tea cloth until all are ready.

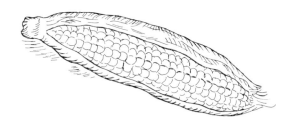

GARLIC BREAD NUGGETS

SERVES 4

Most people enjoy the taste of garlic but there are some who are allergic to it. Substitute minced onion if this is the case.

1 small rectangular fresh wholemeal loaf	¼ teaspoon salt
6–8 cloves garlic	150 ml (¼ pint) best quality olive oil.

Pre-heat the oven to gas mark 5, 375°F (190°C).

Cut the top crust from the length of the loaf and set aside. Pull out walnut-size balls of the soft bread and put into a large bowl.

Peel the garlic and crush with the salt on a small piece of foil until the juices run. Tip into a jug, add the olive oil, beat thoroughly, then pour evenly over the bread pieces, tossing to coat.

Spread out on a baking sheet and bake for 15 minutes, turning the bread balls over once during cooking to brown evenly.

Pack the balls into the empty loaf, cover with the crust lid and bake for 10–15 minutes.

Remove the bread balls with a fork and spoon and serve in the quantity desired. Reserve the crusts to make garlic flavoured dried bread crumbs.

HOT CHEESE WAFFLES

SERVES 4

Waffles should be cooked in a waffle iron but I have tried this recipe in a steel, non-stick, electric sandwich contact grill and while the appearance is less attractive, the taste remains the same.

225 g (8 oz) plain flour
3 eggs
300 ml (½ pint) milk
½ teaspoon white pepper
100 g (4 oz) polyunsaturated

margarine or softened butter
175 g (6 oz) grated Gruyère cheese

sunflower oil for coating waffle iron

Put all the ingredients except the cheese in a food processor and blend until smooth – the mixture should be thick enough to coat the back of a spoon. Stir in the cheese.

Heat a waffle iron and brush sparingly on both sides with oil.

Two-thirds fill with the batter and cook for 2–3 minutes until browned. Turn the waffle iron over half-way through cooking.

Open the waffle iron, ease out the waffle with a round-bladed knife if necessary, then cook the other waffles in the same way.

Serve hot with butter, a savoury sauce, a vegetable topping or as a main course accompaniment.

SESAME SEED CHEESE DUMPLINGS

SERVES 4

Dumplings should be light. Unless directed, do not keep them waiting too long before cooking. Never allow the cooking liquid to boil and eat them freshly made rather than re-heated. However, when you come home at the end of a hard day's work and have to have your stew re-heated, these dumplings will still be appetising if not at their peak.

175 g (6 oz) self-raising flour
1 teaspoon baking powder
pinch of salt
75 g (3 oz) butter or margarine

2 tablespoons sesame seeds
2 tablespoons grated hard cheese
  e.g. Parmesan or Cheddar

Sift the flour, baking powder and salt into a mixing bowl and rub in the butter or margarine until the mixture resembles breadcrumbs. Stir in the sesame seeds and cheese.

Add 4 tablespoons cold water and mix with a fork to a soft dough, adding extra water if necessary. It is better to have the dough too soft rather than too firm.

Turn on to a lightly floured surface and roll with the hands into a sausage shape. Cut into 10 or 12 and shape gently into balls with floured hands.

Cook as required in stews or casseroles.

For a meal-in-one soup, bring plenty of well-flavoured stock to the boil and add the dumplings one by one. As soon as they rise to the surface cover the pan with a lid, reduce the heat and cook for 20 minutes.

TRICORN PUFFS

MAKES 32

These savoury puff pastry triangles can be eaten as a snack with drinks, as a garnish or as an accompaniment to casseroles, stews or highly sauced main courses. They are versatile and, as they open during baking to reveal the filling, they are also very attractive.

225 g (8 oz) ready-to-roll puff pastry
2 tablespoons Marmite or similar
  yeast extract

75 g (3 oz) grated Cheddar cheese
½ beaten egg
¼ teaspoon salt

Cut the pastry into two and roll out each half on a floured surface to a 23 cm (9 in) square.

Brush one half with Marmite, taking care not to stretch the pastry and sprinkle with two-thirds of the cheese. Place the other pastry square on top and roll out gently until the pastry square measures 25 cm (10 in). Trim the edges with a sharp knife.

Beat the egg and salt together with ½ teaspoon cold water and brush over the surface.

Cut into four equal strips, then cut each strip into four squares and divide each into two triangles. Sprinkle with the remaining cheese. Place the pastry pieces well apart on two buttered baking trays and refrigerate for 30 minutes until chilled.

Meanwhile pre-heat the oven to gas mark 7, 425°F (220°C).

Place the baking tray in the centre of the oven and bake for 10 minutes until golden brown and serve warm. The puffs can be re-heated in the oven for 3–4 minutes.

INDEX

Index

159